Safety for the Service Technician

Hazards on the Job Site and How to Protect Yourself

Jerry Isenhour
Robby Murphy

Table of Contents

Introduction

"Safety stuff" is something every home services technician and professional encounters on a daily basis. It is something we can all agree is essential, both at work and in our personal lives.

This manual was developed from an online class in the CVC Virtual Academy. A lot of time and thought was put into creating the class, and it was our goal to provide as thorough as possible an overview of the kinds of safety concerns we face daily in the field. Some of this comes from having personally experienced what can happen when safety is not a top priority or is overlooked, some comes from what has happened to employees and to fellow service professionals.

Although we come from the world of chimney sweep and service technicians, this has been written to appeal to all kinds of blue-collar home service professionals; safety is not particular to one type of profession.

In this manual, we will review things like personal protective equipment, fall protection, common airborne hazards, proper care and use of tools, and even personal health habits, like rest, hydration, and nutrition, that contribute to being able to perform at your best in the field. Part of performing at your best is being mentally sharp, so how you treat your body *off* the job has a significant impact on your performance *on* the job.

Of course, no one plans to get injured. But we can develop bad habits, skipping safety procedures, particularly when doing the same work over and over. It's easy to rationalize, 'it won't make a difference, just this once.' And as bad as it is to be injured, as an employer your heart just drops when it happens to one of your team. It is our hope that employers will use this course to develop standard operating procedures (SOPs) for job site safety, and employees will use this course to improve their ability to protect themselves and their co-workers.

This manual is intended to be used both as a stand-alone guide and as a complement to the *Safety Review For a Service Technician* class offered in the CVC Virtual Academy. Subscribers to the CVC Virtual Academy can access this course as part of their subscription. Non-subscribers can find the course at www.safetyreviewforaservicetechnician.com at the price of $69.00. The information contained here aligns section-by-section with the virtual class so that, while participating in the class, you can follow along in this manual. Hearing and seeing the information together reinforces it and improves retention. It is our hope that this will "raise the bar" on job-site safety practices across a variety of service and construction fields.

Our mission in the production of this book is to assist in the prevention of accidents and fatalities and it should be issued to every technician as a go-to reference for safe work habits and practices. We dedicate this book to the blue-collar home service industry - you are the work force that provides consumers with the specialty services they need to properly maintain and enhance their homes. This type of service is only available in person; it cannot be bought online, which makes your expertise even more desirable and important.

Chapter 1: Strategies for Avoiding Injury

How to Make it Home at the End of the Day

Every person who runs a business is concerned with profit, right? It doesn't make sense to operate a business unless you can turn a profit. And part of that is making sure your team is working at its most efficient and effective on every job.

A big part of maintaining your profits, efficiency, and effectiveness is avoiding injuries and fatalities. How efficient is it to have to stop work to deal with even a minor injury, let alone the nightmare scenario of someone being seriously injured, or even killed? And it certainly doesn't improve your profitability to have to undergo an OSHA review of a workplace incident. Nor does a large OSHA fine improve the profit picture for the business!

While you may not consciously be aware of it, your number one goal as a worker is each day is to make it home to your family and loved ones. That goes for employers and employees alike.

Most of us spend as much time with our co-workers as we do our own family; we work eight, ten, twelve hours a day, 5 (or more) days a week. That's a lot of time, and those relationships are important. The emotional toll of seeing someone you employ, or even work with, suffer a catastrophic injury or be killed is tremendous. Plus, as an employer, there is going to be the burden of responsibility – could I have done something to prevent this? Did I have all the systems in place to protect my people?

What we do carries risk, more than in many other professions. It is on us – employers and employees – to make sure we carry this mindset of safety through our day, every day. Accidents are called accidents for a reason. But virtually every accident can be prevented.

Preventing Accidents

We all accept that 'accidents happen'. Well, yes, they do. But we believe that EVERY accident or misstep can be prevented. Every fall, cut, bruise, even every time you get debris in your eye – can be prevented.

It starts by thinking ahead. What is going to happen once you start your next action? What can happen once you have that tool in your hand? When sparks start flying – literally – what could happen? A key skill in prevention of injury is the ability to anticipate what could go wrong and taking the proper action steps to prevent and things from happening.

Safety means thinking ahead, thinking before you act. Again, you need to develop the skill of anticipation. Before anything happens on a job site, consider the consequences of that action. This doesn't have to be onerous, and it doesn't mean you should be paralyzed by the possibilities. But it does mean that you need to know what could go wrong, and have a plan to prevent it.

Why Do Accidents Happen?

Preventing every accident seems impossible: how could you foresee and avoid EVERY potential problem, protect yourself and your employees from EVERY eventuality? While that is certainly our goal, we all fall short sometimes. But there are things we can do to achieve our goal of an accident-free workplace.

#1 There is no system

Do you have safety protocols in place? Do they cover all of your processes, tools, and services? A quick "be careful" when the crew pulls out in the morning is not a safety system. Making sure every crew member knows how to remove the ladder from the work vehicle and set it up correctly is important, but they also need to know how to determine the best location to set the ladder, how to look for and avoid hazards (like electrical service lines), how to climb a ladder, how to transition from the ladder to the roof (and back again), and how to carry tools or equipment on the ladder. And that's just one small aspect of what most of us do on a daily basis. This process requires training, not just at the start of someone's employment, but ongoing, continuous training to combat the consequences of bad things happening. Even the most skilled veterans need regularly scheduled refreshers on safety training.

Every procedure needs to have a written protocol for how it is to be done. Every tool needs a written description of how the tool is to be used, stored, and maintained. If you don't have these written down, they may as well not exist, and you don't truly have a system. If it is not documented, then you have a hole in your safety plan. A **system** is a set of safety protocols that clearly describes what needs to be done in a given situation. It arms all your employees with the knowledge they require to perform their daily work correctly and safely.

If you do not have these systems in place, it may seem like an impossible task to pull them all together. There is a saying – 'how do you eat an elephant? One bite at a time'. You will not be able to create an entire safety system in a weekend. But you can start today. Jerry Isenhour's book, "Standardizing Standard Operating Procedures" is an excellent resource and guide for developing the systems your business needs to create safety protocols. We also highly recommend looking at the manuals that Al Levi has composed; you can take a look at his systems by going to the following link: www.7powercontractor.com/cvc. If you are just starting to develop your systems, or if you have some in place but have procrastinated on completing them, these manuals will set you on the right path.

#2 The system is wrong

So, you have safety protocols in place. Your employees have read them. An accident happens.

Your safety protocols may be wrong. They may not cover what they need to cover, they may not cover it completely, or they are just plain incorrect.

This can be a shock: 'but I did what I was supposed to do, how could this happen?' I well remember after a fatality the owner saying to me, "I never thought someone could be killed from a fall from a ladder." This launched the owner onto a path of education in how to prevent injuries from a fall. It is almost easier to have no systems in place than to have the wrong ones. But this is also a great learning opportunity. If you ever interview someone after an accident, you can almost always trace the accident back to where a mistake was made. We refer to this as a postmortem inspection. In hindsight, it is often very easy to see the turning point, the moment when the accident became likely, even inevitable. Don't beat yourself up; instead, use that information to improve your systems.

#3 Someone did not follow the system

Usually, people do not willfully ignore safety directions. It is far more likely that a failure to follow a protocol is caused by the person not understanding the system or not having been properly trained in the system. If someone doesn't know what the right thing is, how can they be expected to do it?

It's not enough to train your staff. You have to communicate the information so they will comprehend it. Some people learn better by listening, some by reading, and some by doing. Your training needs to take these learning differences into account if it is to be a truly successful program.

The employer must also take the steps of both accountability and documenting these incidents and the warnings that were issued to the employee. If bad things do happen, having documented warnings is going to be critical during the OSHA or other inspections and/or reviews your company may have to undergo.

Part of your employee training should be that all accidents or injuries need to be reported to management immediately. As the employer, you need to know everything about what happened; you may have to file a report with OSHA, your insurance company, or other entity. The person completing the report must have all the facts at hand and be able to document the information on any reporting form required.

It is easy to overlook or shortchange your training programs. Many tasks seem obvious, and many safety procedures do as well. Often, we are hiring people to fill an urgent need, and want to get them in the field yesterday. We rely on the current employees to train the new ones (even though we don't always tell them that that is the plan), and expect that they know the proper way to do it. We rely on the 'learn by doing' method. All this means is we are putting untrained or undertrained people in the field, representing us. This almost always costs us in the long run. A great technician will not automatically be a great trainer; teaching and doing are different skill sets. Simply being able to do a job does not qualify someone as a trainer.

Even when we hire people who have some experience, either in our trade or one that is similar to ours, we cannot assume they know how WE want things done, or if they can perform in a safe manner. We don't know how, or even if, they were trained in the past. We don't know what kind of bad habits were taught and reinforced in their previous jobs. We may have to overcome bad teaching, and we may encounter resistance when we do that. But if an employee wants to stay with your company and be successful, they will listen as long as they are being taught properly.

The other thing to consider is that training isn't a 'one and done' proposition. New tools and new concepts are being developed all the time, so even our veterans need time set aside for training. For example, in the last few years we've seen an increase in the focus on fall protection. Do you now require employees to wear helmets? Do they have to be harnessed and secured for work off the ground? Do they all know how to check the fit of their helmet, or their harness? Do they know when those things are required? In 'the good old days', very few companies paid attention to fall protection; you may have heard about it, but almost never actually did anything about it. We all have heard about companies that have experienced a serious loss due to injury, or even death, from a lack of proper fall protection, and the trades overall have become much more aware and willing to use the equipment that will help protect us. We are starting to do the right thing, and we need to be sure we do the right thing the right way. Which means we need to be training on it, from the newest worker to the boss.

Short Term Injuries, Long Term Health

When we talk about short-term injuries, we are referring to things like a simple cut or bruise, a sprain, getting something in your eye. These may require some time away from the job, but generally don't lead to hospital stays or lengthy recoveries. That's not to say there aren't any long-term consequences – repeatedly spraining an ankle can lead to a chronic problem or weakness.

Sometimes we aren't even talking about a specific injury. When we are young and bold, we can abuse our bodies to a certain extent and bounce back. But repeatedly abusing ourselves can cause cumulative effects and all of a sudden, you're in your 50's and need a new hip or a new knee, you need ongoing physical therapy, or cortisone injections, just to have a functional body.

So, it's important to take care of your body at times and all ages, not just after the damage has been done. Work in the trades is not for the weak. Our daily work demands a lot of our bodies; there is a lot of repetitive motion as well as just plain hard work. If you want to be able to move that ladder or carry those tools when you're 50 or 60, you need to take care of your body for decades before that. If you want to be able to enjoy life when you're older, play with your grandkids or engage in physical hobbies, you need to set yourself up for that now. Nobody wants to spend their "golden years" confined to a wheelchair or dependent on a cane just to get around.

One of us had a fall from a ladder at the beginning of his career. To this day, he experiences pain that is debilitating to the point that he can barely walk at times without the assistance of a cane. Sitting for extended periods of time, like flying or riding in a car, can bring it on. The muscles seem to 'freeze up' and leave him barely able to get around. He was young and careless and had one accident 35 years ago that, to this day, causes problems that reduce his quality of life. Don't be like him

Short Term v. Long Term Exposure

Injury doesn't just refer to falls or missteps. For example, many of us work with toxic chemicals, like sulphur. If you draw a big whiff of soot or other toxic materials into your lungs, it can shut your system down for a minute – you literally can't breathe. That is an acute effect.

Now, think about doing that repeatedly over the course of your career. You are creating chronic exposure, and causing chronic injury. For example, sulphur, when mixed with moisture, turns into sulfuric acid in your lungs. So, the aggregation of acute effects (each time you breathe it in) creates a chronic, long-term injury or effect. And the more often you're exposed, the longer that substance is going to be in your body.

Sulphur is not the only hazardous airborne material we encounter. Our work frequently exposes us to particulate that we should not be inhaling or ingesting. A big part of personal protection is avoiding breathing in these materials; we don't just need to watch out for falls or misuse of tools; we need to protect ourselves from the 'invisible' hazards too.

NOTES:

____

____

____

____

____

____

____

____

____

____

____

____

____

Chapter 2: Health & Risk

Long-term Respiratory Risks

In various trades and service industries, you're going to be dealing with a lot of chemicals, including organic materials that are known to be carcinogenic (cancer causing). The damage from these can be insidious. If you aren't wearing a proper respirator, you can feel fine now, but you go home and cough up some black stuff from your lungs or blow it out of your nose. You may swallow soot and other airborne particles, which then end up in your stomach.

You may think that, since you coughed this stuff up, or blew your nose well, you've gotten rid of it. The problem is it can already have caused damage. The damage from a single exposure is not likely to give you cancer, but think about doing it five (or more) days a week, fifty weeks a year, for decades. This could damage your lungs. This could cause issues with your heart. Cancer is becoming more and more treatable, but sometimes it isn't, and it could take your life when you are still relatively young. Statistically, the rates of lung, esophageal, pancreas, colon, and bladder cancer are higher in chimney sweeps than the general population. Over one million construction and general industry workers are exposed to asbestos annually. Welders, painters, mechanics, and people working in the mining and milling industries have higher-than-average cancer rates when compared to the general population.

Soot doesn't have to enter your body to harm you. Scrotal cancer used to be called "chimney sweep's cancer" or "soot wart" because it was so prevalent in Europe in the 18th century. It is actually a type of skin cancer that forms on the exterior of the scrotum.

It is possible to develop respiratory issues significant enough that they start to reduce your quality of life. Do you want to be able to climb a flight or two of stairs in your 50's? Do you want to be able to play with your grandkids, or just sit on the sideline and watch? Inhaled particulate, like soot, can worsen asthma, it can limit your ability to participate in everyday activities.

We all see people on job sites who won't wear a respirator, even in situations where they exposed to large quantities of toxins and carcinogens. They may be fine; they may live to a ripe old age without a problem. But it is more likely that they are going find their quality of life diminished in some way by the choice to not prevent carcinogenic materials from getting into their body.

Taking precautions, like always wearing respirators when there is any sort of prolonged exposure – and wearing them properly – can significantly cut down on what you are ingesting over the short and long haul. The minor inconvenience of using precautions can reap tremendous benefits for you now and, more importantly, in the future. It could literally save your life. Don't wait for the bad thing to happen before you take action – do it now.

Nutrition & Hydration

Remember mom nagging you to 'eat your veggies', or reminding you that 'breakfast is the most important meal of the day'? Well, she wasn't wrong.

Our crew stops at the local deli in the morning to get a solid breakfast. We keep apples, bananas, and other fruit in the shop for snacks (we have some candy too, because who doesn't love candy?).

One of the authors learned he was diabetic. That made him look into the dangers of sugar in his diet. It is not easily digestible, it can cause liver disease (and as we already knew, diabetes), and it can even contribute to heart disease. That's not to say you have to eliminate all sugar from your diet – just make it a treat, rather than a main element of your diet.

A balanced diet includes vegetables, fruits, lean proteins, whole grains, healthy fats, and liquids. Eating a healthy diet not only makes it easier to stay focused on the job and have the energy you need to get through the day, it also maximizes your odds of living a long and healthy life. A person can't get through days at work on high sugar drinks and candy bars for long. They taste good, and you get a 'sugar buzz' that makes you feel energized. But what goes up must come down – a short time after the buzz comes the crash. Then you need more sugar to keep going. Buzz – crash – buzz – crash…it's no way to get through the day, to say nothing of how poorly you perform while that's happening.

Energy drinks are not hydration. Coffee, Mountain Dew®, and Coca Cola® are not hydration. Hydration is WATER. Hydration gets the body what it needs. You cannot function in your optimal state if you are dehydrated.

Thirst is not actually a good indicator of whether you are becoming dehydrated. Frequently, you are already well into a state of dehydration before you feel thirsty. You need to take in fluids like water or Gatorade® regularly, all day long, to be properly hydrated.

Dehydration causes such symptoms as fatigue, dizziness, and confusion. None of that sounds like something you want to be experiencing up on a roof, going up and down a ladder, operating heavy machinery or power tools, or driving your work vehicle.

We often are not aware of how much water we are losing during the day, through sweat or respiration. Consider a hot, dry day. We may be sweating, but it is evaporating off our skin so quickly we can't really tell how much we're losing. Every time you breathe, you are losing moisture. So even if it's freezing cold, you are still dehydrating yourself, and you still need to replace that water for your body to function optimally.

Now, your employer can't make you make good choices. They can't force you to eat a good breakfast, or make you put down the Red Bull®. This is up to you. You only get one body in this lifetime; you've got to maintain it and keep it functioning properly.

Proper Sleep & Rest

It's simple – without proper sleep and rest, your mind doesn't function correctly, your mood is off, you become irritable, and you are more easily distracted.

Getting the proper rest includes getting up and starting your day right. Pushing the 'snooze' button until 5 minutes before you have to leave the house means you aren't going to be properly prepared to face the day.

We all know coworkers who have to drag themselves into work in the morning, they're just drained. It's because they went out the night before, maybe didn't get to bed until late, maybe had a little too much to drink, maybe once they got to bed they had trouble falling asleep.

Get to bed at a decent hour, make sure you're comfortable – the room isn't too hot or cold, turn the lights off, use a white noise machine if you live in a place with a lot of going on outside. Get up early enough to gather your thoughts, eat a healthy breakfast, exercise or do some stretching – in short, get your body ready for the day. If you aren't getting a decent nights' sleep, you may find yourself dozing off behind the wheel, or having trouble staying focused on the job site. This is how accidents can happen.

Some folks suffer from sleep apnea; this is when breathing stops periodically during the night. Its symptoms include daytime fatigue and snoring; this snoring is usually louder than 'regular' snoring, and can include long pauses between breaths, gasping, or choking. If you have a partner, you will know if you snore! This is a potentially dangerous condition. At its worst, it can cause heart and blood pressure problems. It is often caused by being overweight, and affects men more than women.

Treatment ranges from lifestyle changes, like losing weight, quitting smoking, and treating nasal allergies to use of a CPAP (continuous positive airway pressure) device. Getting sleep apnea under control isn't just better for your health overall; by allowing you to truly get a decent night's sleep, it reduces the risk of injury on the job.

NOTES:

____

____

____

____

____

____

____

____

____

____

Chapter 3: Assessing the Job Site

Job Site Assessment

One of the things that most folks in the trades discover is that, after we've been doing this for a while, we find ourselves looking at properties as we drive by. Not just the ones we are hired to service; any place we see that needs repairs or major overhauls. For those of you who are just starting out, see if that doesn't happen to you!

When it comes to assessing a job site, let's start from the very beginning. Where do you park? Don't park on the lawn, stay away from the patio; in general, look around and make sure you're in a spot where a) you can exit and enter the service vehicle safely, b) you aren't potentially damaging the customer's property, and c) you aren't blocking someone who is going to need to get out of there before your work is complete.

As you come onto your customer's property, remember the phrase "a man's (or woman's) home is their castle". This is their haven. This is where they live, where they raise their family, this is the place they love. Don't step on things you shouldn't step on. Some people take enormous pride in their lawn, and you start off on the wrong foot right away if you tread on it or, even worse, drive on it.

This may sound funny, but you've got to locate the particular area of the house you are to service. If, for example, you are there to work on the chimney, you will find that some are on the back side of the house, and may not be visible as you approach the house or from the driveway. There may be more than one chimney (not every homeowner can tell you how many chimneys they have or where they are located). If you are working on the roof, make sure you know where the homeowner means for you to work: are you doing all of the main building's roof, are you working on the garage or outbuilding roof? Are you painting the whole house, or only a portion?

Will the job require you to be on the roof? You need to find the best - and safest - access point. Walk around the house; the spot closest to the driveway (and your van) may not always be the best place to set a ladder. Roof access from the back of the house may be vastly better than from the front. There may be an addition with a lower roof that provides an easy way to get to the main roof and any secondary roofs you will be working on.

While you're doing this, do NOT climb through their flower beds, crush their shrubbery, or otherwise cause damage. If you must work around plantings, notify the owner and discuss with them how to approach the work. Sometimes you can't avoid shrubs or flowers, but bringing the homeowner into the conversation and working out a plan of attack with them is better than having them walk outside to find you've set your ladder in the middle of Aunt Millie's prize roses.

Pictures Pictures Pictures. Get before and after pictures of everything, recording from the same location; don't be stingy. One great aspect of digital photography is that you aren't going to run out of film, so get it all. Photograph the exterior of the house; walk all the way around, taking pictures of all the possible access points to the roof. Where does the electrical service come into the house? Take pictures of the driveway; are you going to be limited in how many work vehicles can park there? Are there power lines that are going to dictate where you set your ladder, staging, or lift? If you have a drone, use it. Get photos from above, not just of the area on which you are working, but of the path from the ladder to it.

Photograph the path from the door through which you will enter the house to the room where the work is being done. Photograph the 'work room' extensively; you want to be aware of things like white furniture, antiques, chotchkes on the mantel, lamps, area rugs, all of it.

This is especially important if the person who is responsible for writing the proposal is not coming to the customer's house. They have to rely on the field notes and the photographs; make sure they have what they need. In the "good old days" we frequently relied just on notes and that led to mistakes, or leaving out important parts of the proposal, because the writer didn't have the information they needed. It is such an easy thing to fix; you just need to make sure you follow through. The pictures you take should allow the person writing the proposal to anticipate and address any problem that could occur. Sometimes we miss things; no one is perfect. But you are always shooting for 100%, and that includes anticipating where things could go wrong.

All of this will not only be invaluable when writing a proposal, it will also confirm the condition of the house, yard, gardens, and driveway BEFORE the work commenced. It's not fun to be accused of damaging the gutters, ripping up the lawn, or staining the carpet when you know they were damaged when you got there. It's even worse when you can't prove it – so document document document.

The job starts with an assessment – not just of the property, but of safety. Federal guidelines require that safety assessments be completed for every job. Commercial job sites almost always have an 'all hands on deck' safety meeting before a job begins. It gets all the various contractors on the same page, and avoids conflict and confusion, all of which helps reduce risk.

When you begin your safety assessment, look at the photographs of the exterior of the home: is there a paved and/or tiled area in front of the house? Are you going to set a ladder there? Probably not; you can't secure it without damaging the pavement or tile, and it could slide out from under you.

Are there plantings around the house's foundation? Where are those located? Is there a point where you can gain roof access and avoid the shrubbery and flower beds? If not, can you minimize your interaction with them? Are there underground structures, like a septic tank, that could be damaged by heavy equipment? You will want to have that area carefully marked for you before the job begins.

Are there poisonous plants? What about cactus? We have seen someone set a ladder right next to a cactus and, when he came down, he brushed up against it. He ended up with dozens of cactus needles in his posterior. He was in horrible pain, and had to seek medical help to have them removed. In case you don't know this, cactus needles or spines are similar to fish hooks; you can't just pull them out, at least not without inflicting even more damage.

As an example, consider the interior of this house. Did you notice that

there is a fair amount of light-colored furniture? There is what looks like a fragile vase sitting on the hearth, right in front of the fireplace, as well as several large decorative items on the mantel, none of which appear to be very secure. And there's a glass coffee table; that would be easy to damage. The floors and the area rug are beautiful and appear to be well maintained. All of these things need to be moved; at a minimum, the furniture needs to be covered and covered well. Ask the homeowner to take every breakable item out of the room. Say you're installing a new liner or insert in the fireplace, or replacing windows, doors, or light fixtures. Any of these jobs can create airborne debris, and you have to be prepared. If the furniture can't leave the room, it should at least be moved as far from the work area as possible. You want space to work, and you don't want to upset your customer by ruining their brand-new sofa. If you are going to be spraying anything, make sure you protect walls as well as furnishings. You do not want to have to redo the white fireplace mantel and surround, or replace a portion of the hardwood floor, because your overspray stained or damaged it.

There are a lot of things to keep in mind as you prepare for a job. If you're the team leader, you need to be aware of and have a plan for addressing all these concerns. You also need to communicate all of this to your team, and make sure they understand the particulars of the job site and what safety measures you expect them to take. If you fail to do this, frankly, you are derelict in your duties. If you're there alone, you want to make sure these concerns are at the top of your mind, that you don't get careless or start thinking 'I've done hundreds of these, I'm just fine'.

So – you've taken all your pictures, made note of all the potential pitfalls, and the customer has hired you. If there are multiple people on the job, we encourage you to have a pre-job planning meeting. Discuss things like placement of your roof access, be it ladders, staging, or a lift. Can you maneuver the lift without tearing up the lawn or, even worse, crushing a septic tank? You want their home – inside and out – to look undisturbed after you're gone.

We've gone over protecting the homeowner's property; now we're going to talk about protecting YOU. We will review the various kinds of protective gear; there are a lot, and they are all important.

NOTES:

Chapter 4: Protecting Yourself

Respirator Fit Testing

We will start with respirators. If you've been in the trades long enough, you probably know someone who, for whatever reason, just won't wear a respirator. You may also be aware that that has caused health issues for that person, things that possibly could have been avoided if they'd worn a respirator properly and consistently.

There are two types of respirators:

negative pressure (left) and positive pressure (right). Negative pressure respirators are more common, probably because they are less expensive.

Whatever type you use, it is important that it filters out organic matter as well as fumes. There are carcinogenic substances in our workplaces. Also, many tradespeople use chemicals in their work, and those fumes should not be inhaled.

A negative pressure respirator only works if it fits. It must be fit-tested to each individual, and the fit needs to be checked regularly. It has to conform to the contours of your face. If you are clean-shaven but come to work with stubble, those little hairs are going to create leakage spots in the seal. Properly fitting one to a guy with a full beard is more difficult, and sometimes impossible.

In order to test whether a respirator is properly fitted, it needs to be put on, then powder is sprayed around the edges of the respirator. That shows where the leaks are; you need to re-fit and re-test it until there is no powder making its way into the respirator.

The rubber gasket that creates the seal will degrade over time, and when that happens, that respirator can no longer provide a tight seal and should be replaced.

If you aren't using respirators now, or aren't pressure testing them regularly, get some and start using and testing them. Make sure you are protecting yourself and your employees.

As an aside – the reason Adolf Hitler wore that odd little mustache was a failed gas mask. He had a fuller moustache in World War I; his mask leaked and he suffered mustard gas poisoning. So, for the remainder of his life, he maintained that little mustache that didn't extend to the edges of his mouth.

So, you or your crew wear full beards and can't seem to get a proper seal with a negative pressure respirator. Do you surrender to the idea that you will just not be able to protect yourselves? No – you use a positive pressure respirator.

The positive pressure type respirator has a full-face mask, as you see in the picture above. So, the positive pressure respirator also functions as eye protection, as well as protecting your head from absorption of debris and particulates. They work by use of a blower system, with filters that are mounted on your belt or back. The air passes through the filters and is pumped into the respirator.

Although they are more expensive than a negative pressure respirator, it's important to look at the positive pressure respirators as an investment. Say you are working on a major restoration or construction project, with tons of dust and particulate everywhere. You are being exposed to some very undesirable materials, and you're being exposed to them a lot. Add in the fact that you have facial hair that doesn't allow a negative pressure respirator to make a good seal on your face. You really have to use a respirator, and you have to use one that will work on your face. There are certain areas where you may be tempted to cut corners, which we never encourage, but it is never acceptable when it comes to safety equipment and PPE.

We should note here that it's not a great idea to pass a respirator around. Every person on your crew should have their own, and they should check them regularly for defects or damage. If they are negative pressure, they also need to check the fit often.

As noted above, a positive pressure respirator also protects you from absorption of soot through the skin on your head. In some Scandinavian countries, chimney sweep offices are required to have saunas, and sweeps are required to use them at set intervals. The sauna opens the pores, so the soot and other particulates that have been absorbed by the skin gets out.

Respirators, negative or positive, need to be stored and transported properly. They can't be tossed into the back of the van, or hung on a hook behind the driver's seat. They have to be stored in something that will keep them clean. What's the point of wearing something specifically so you won't inhale particulates, then leaving it laying around in a space that's loaded with them? All that junk you're trying to keep out of your lungs will end on up the inside of your respirator, where you're just going to suck it all into your lungs. Your respirator should be cleaned regularly, it should be sanitized, and it should be stored in a container that protects it from contamination. The filters need to be cleaned or replaced regularly. Keep a large supply of filter cartridges and covers on hand, organized and stored so they are protected just as the respirators are, and label them so every member of your crew can locate theirs easily. Treat them like one of your tools – because they are. If you take care of them, they will take care of you.

Soot and Creosote

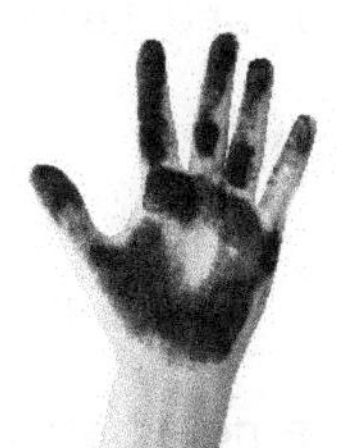

If you are a chimney sweep, an oil burner technician or an installer that deals with connector pipes and heating systems, soot and creosote are just a part of the job. You are going to be exposed, regularly and frequently. While this is primarily an issue for sweeps, any repair or renovation work you do in or around a chimney can bring you into contact with these substances.

Soot and creosote are carcinogenic. They can be absorbed through your respiratory system as well as through your skin.

Now, if you took a handful of soot and rubbed it all up and down your arms, then washed it off, you'd probably be just fine. But if you did it five days a week, fifty or more weeks a year, for decades, you're going to have health problems. You need to protect your body – all of it.

Most of us wear gloves, so our hands are protected. But the rest of our skin can absorb this stuff too. We need to protect our face, arms, legs, and torso. Your skin should not come in contact with this stuff.

Creosote is found in a few forms: soot; a hard, almost glassy looking material; or something that resembles black bubble gum or popcorn. Regardless of the form, you do not want to have it touching your skin, you don't want to inhale it; secure it in a container and get it out of the house. Whenever there's a chance of it becoming airborne, your vacuum should be nearby, and probably running. When dealing with it outside, anywhere really, keep it off your tools, away from the inside of your truck's cab area, and keep it contained, then dispose of it properly.

Silica Dust

Soot and creosote are not the only airborne materials you should be concerned about. Ever dump a bag of mortar into a mixer, and get engulfed in a cloud? Or have to cut masonry materials? That's silica dust.

Whenever you are cutting, bending or breaking materials, or using a grinder, you are often releasing silica dust into the air around you. You should not be exposing yourself to this; it can cause cement poisoning. And you don't have to inhale it to have problems – it can enter through your skin. When you dump the mortar into the mixer, it's not enough to hold your breath; you actually have to cover yourself, so there is no exposed skin, and you have your respirator on throughout the process as well.

A few decades ago, no one thought about silica dust being hazardous. It's only recently that we've been made aware of the health risks. So even though the 'old-timers' have never heard of it, it's a real issue and you need to protect yourself.

Asbestos

Back in the 1940's and 50's, asbestos was a commonly-used insulating material. As a siding material, it was frequently sold to homeowners as a way to insulate their homes without having to open or remove walls. It is not in use today, but if your customer base includes homes that are 70, 80, or more years old, you may encounter it.

If you are a regular TV watcher, you have most likely seen ads from multiple attorneys, seeking victims of asbestos exposure to join class-action lawsuits. Asbestos can cause a variety of cancers, including mesothelioma, lung cancer, ovarian cancer, and laryngeal cancer. It can also cause asbestosis, COPD, pleural plaques, pleural thickening, pleural effusion, and atelectasis. We can't even pronounce some of these, but we are sure I don't want to suffer from any of them!

Although the primary path through which asbestos enters the body in by inhalation, it can also be ingested, or enter through the skin. The fibers are so fine as to not be visible, so you could breathe them in, or have them land on your lunch or your skin, and you would never know.

We have encountered asbestos in the field. In one case, the whole chimney appeared to be constructed from asbestos, with a clay flue liner. There was a fake-brick housing above the roof that was made of what I assumed was asbestos. We have encountered large connector pipes at a commercial facility that were completely encased in asbestos insulation. You are not supposed to touch asbestos; if you encounter it on a job, inform the homeowner that they need to locate someone licensed in asbestos removal and mitigation. Not only are they trained in how to handle it, they will use the appropriate disposal techniques – you can't just toss this stuff in the landfill.

Chemicals

In addition to creosote, soot, silica dust, and asbestos, much of our materials arsenal contains potentially hazardous chemicals. They may be in a powder form, a liquid, a spray, and we need to know what we are dealing with and what the proper procedures are for their use.

We use things like water-proofers, cement sealers, crown coats, adhesives, spray foam insulation, chimney flue resurfacing materials, spray paint, even bee and wasp repellent. At least, a lot of these types of items are stored in our work vans, so even if we aren't actively using them, we have the potential for exposure.

Sometimes, we can have some significant reactions to a product that is being used as intended. We may be allergic, or not using it correctly. Even personal products can cause problems that, while they are not caused by the work environment, carry over and affect the people we are working with. In the past, we had a crew member who was quite hairy – people would call him 'gorilla man'. So, one day he decides he wants to do something about this, so what does he do? He grabs his wife's Nair and spreads it all over his back. It wasn't long before he started having a bad reaction – the skin was actually coming off! And that was a product that was meant for that use.

Protecting yourself is critical. If you are working with known toxic or harmful chemicals, wear your respirator, gloves, goggles, a Tyvek suit –

the works. You want to do everything right in terms of protecting yourself from all kinds of chemical exposures.

COVID-19

In the beginning of 2020, we had no idea what we were about to experience. COVID-19 changed our world.

Who doesn't have a mask for COVID today? When this started, we learned we needed to keep 'social distance' from people, be careful what we touched, be aware of symptoms and avoid people when we felt ill. Now, some of those restrictions are starting to lift or be refined; people are getting vaccinated, they're getting booster shots, and we have home test kits so we can check ourselves if we start to exhibit symptoms. But COVID has altered our society, probably for a long time to come. During our team meetings now, we stay six feet apart, and we hold these meetings outside.

Someone reading this in 2030 or in later years may skip right over this section, this may not be part of our culture any more – and wouldn't that be great! But for now, we have to adapt to it, and we have to understand what our customers expect from us. When someone in the company is diagnosed, even if they don't have a serious or dangerous case, it can take a toll on our business. Work has to be rescheduled, some customers may be hesitant to let even people who haven't been diagnosed into their home, just because a coworker could have exposed them. And we have to take a lead from our customers – some will insist on masks, some won't care; some will require everyone coming into their house to be vaccinated, some won't even ask about it.

At this time, all our trucks carry masks and hand sanitizer. We have them in the break room, in the office, and in the training room. We make sure everyone has access to whatever they need to feel prepared and able to put customer's minds at ease.

Eye Protection

Most of us, at one time or another, have had to make a small, quick cut and thought, "I can just squint, it's going to take longer to put on the goggles than make the cut." Sometimes we get away with it. But sometimes, that 'quick cut' sends us to the emergency room. And having metal shavings pulled out with a magnet is not fun. Which is why every member of our crew receives eye protection on Day One.

There are a variety of types of protection. As we saw in the section on respirators, you can have something that does "double duty" – provides protection from inhalants as well as protecting your eyes and face.

Types of Eye Protection:

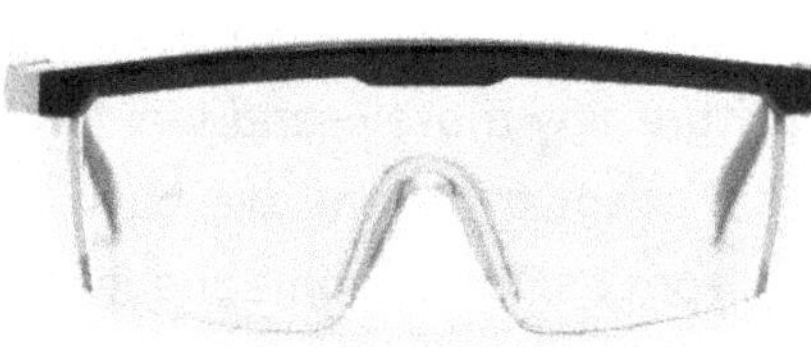

The safety glasses (left) are the minimum type of protection you can use.

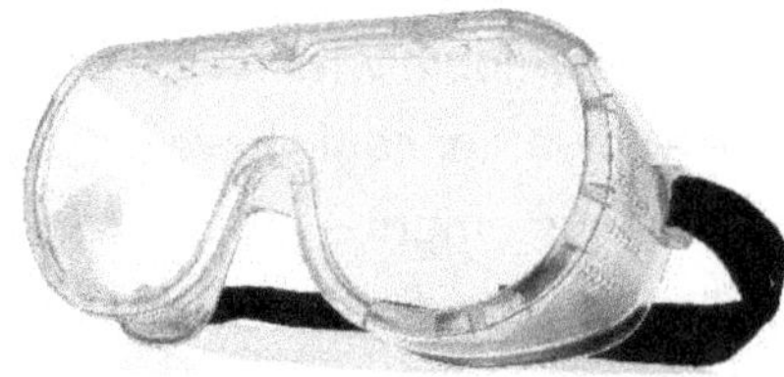

Goggles make a seal with your face, and do an outstanding job; nothing, really, can get in.

The full-face shield is more of a medical type device, but it will also protect your eyes well.

As we said above, who hasn't thought that eye protection wasn't needed 'just this once'? We all do it; we know we shouldn't, but human nature being what it is, we don't like inconvenience and we will take the easy way when we can rationalize it. The truth is, even a quick, one-cut job can cause an injury.

We've been in situations where we ended up in the emergency room, having metal shards removed from an eye. Which, as awful as it sounds, is a temporary injury. You will recover. But sometimes it's a more permanent problem; you can lose an eye through it being impaled by something and being damaged so badly it can't be repaired and, in extreme cases, you can lose your sight completely.

All this goes back to anticipation. Before you proceed on any job, you should be considering what might happen: where are the risks, what are the risks, what can I do to protect myself (and my co-workers) from those risks.

The other important point about eye protection is – you have to keep it clean. You don't want to put on safety goggles that have debris inside them, and have that end up in your eyes. We are starting to see football players wearing more all-encompassing and fuller coverage face shields on their helmets where at one time there was no face shield. Go back even further: the helmet was made of leather with no shock absorbing lining. Race car drivers have gone to full face helmets and a device to protect from neck injuries; much of this is due to catastrophic losses in the sports world. This are just a few examples of how more and more people are recognizing the need to protect their eyes. Make sure you are one of them.

Hearing Protection

Think about the equipment you use every day in your job. Now, think about the level of noise that accompanies it; demolition hammers, nail guns, circular saws, cutting tools – even your vacuum - and consider how close you are to them. And how many hours a day are they running? If you're doing a major construction project, or sweeping 4, 5, 6 chimneys, that could be hours of noise exposure.

The decibel level of our equipment makes using hearing protection critical. There are workers in a variety of trades, who are not that old, who already need hearing aids. You need to protect your hearing whenever you have exposure to noise. Even if it's just 4-5 'whacks' with a hammer on metal – put on that hearing protection. In fact, some of the most damaging sound is percussive – things like driving nails or banging on a pipe section to get it to connect can cause significant hearing loss.

Hearing loss is cumulative; you aren't going to suddenly go deaf from one really loud noise. Exposure, day in and day out, over the course of a career, will cause irreparable damage. The ear muffs (far right image) are the best option, but sometimes the other choices make sense. You should have access to, and use, a variety of hearing protection options.

This doesn't just apply to your life on the job. How loud do you play your music? Have you ever pulled up to a stoplight and the guy next to you is blasting music to the point that your car is vibrating? Can you imagine what that's doing to his hearing?

Do you ride snow machines? Enjoy target shooting? Split firewood? Maybe you're renovating your home, or putting up an outbuilding to house your 'toys'. Hearing protection is important here as well. Your ears don't just suffer from work-based noise; our off-the-job exposure can do just as much damage. Invest in some good quality ear muffs for home and use them!

Head Protection

How many sweeps still wear a top hat on the job? That used to be the chimney sweep's calling card, but it was hardly what you would call a piece of protective equipment. Other tradespeople may not have a particular piece of headwear associated with their work, but are you wearing a baseball cap, or nothing at all?

We know workers who have lost their lives from a simple fall from a ladder. It doesn't need to be a long or hard fall – you don't need to be 30' in the air for a fall to kill you. Without head protection, even a few feet can be enough for brain damage and death. A traditional hard hat isn't designed for fall protection; for that you need a climbing helmet.

A head injury doesn't have to be severe enough to kill you to permanently alter your life. When you hit your head, your brain is jostled and bangs up against your skull. If there is enough force behind that hit, you can have brain damage, damage that is not repairable. You can become disabled, physically, mentally, and emotionally, from a head injury. Is the small amount of inconvenience you go through to put a climbing helmet on greater than the damage you can sustain without one? Personally, we'd rather invest that little extra time and effort, if it means our brains are protected.

Head protection includes more than just from falls. The head sock keeps creosote, soot, and other nasty particulate and chemicals from coming in contact with your scalp or getting in your ears. Do you ever get home at night and start digging soot out of your ears with a Q-tip? Do you think that kind of exposure is innocuous? Better to not let all that junk get into your body in the first place.

Another consideration when it comes to head protection is falling objects. We've all been on job sites where bricks slid off the roof or staging, or a piece of pipe or sheet of plywood slipped out of someone's hand and came crashing down. We'd all like to think we are agile enough to jump out of the way of this projectiles, but wearing a hard hat is a much more reliable way to protect yourself. There's also the matter of running into things. You're thinking about the next step on the job, making the list of tools or materials you need, and the next thing you know you're run smack into the ladder rack that's been dropped to the side of the van. Having that hard hat on is going to make that experience more of an embarrassing moment than one that requires a visit to the emergency room.

One of our clients was working inside a chimney, and the roof guy dropped a rotary hammer from the top of the chimney. It went between the chin strap and got stuck there, but his head was protected. Imagine if he hadn't had his hard hat on, and that hammer had hit him square on. How would his crew have extricated him from that spot? And how would the guy who dropped it, which honestly is a simple mistake any of us could make, feel afterwards?

There isn't a more important part of your body than your brain. Let's make sure it's always protected.

Hand and Arm Protection

Over our careers, we reach into hundreds, maybe thousands, of areas where we can't really see what's going on. Your hands are exposed to all kinds of things, from sharp objects that can scratch or cut, to chemicals that can irritate and burn the skin. We probably expose our hands and arms to more potentially dangerous situations than almost any other part of our bodies.

Scratches may be minor and we often don't even take notice of them. But any opening in the skin is a pathway for infection and disease. The full-arm sleeves offer good protection when we're reaching into a space we can't fully visualize, where we may encounter things that can break or irritate the skin. There are times we're reaching into blind spots during a home renovation, or into thimbles that can be 3-4 feet deep; we certainly can't see where we're putting our hands. Having protective sleeves, as well as gloves, is necessary.

Gloves are your friend, gloves protect you. Heavy, insulated gloves protect you not just from injury but also from exposure in the winter. Who wants to work, or can even work well, with hands that feel like blocks of ice? Thin nitrile gloves, worn under our heavy work gloves, give us some protection even when we have to take the outer gloves off. Sturdy work gloves afford us protection not just from skin irritants or scratches, but from surprise 'visitors' in blind areas on the job site or in a chimney.

Gloves also protect you from developing blisters and calluses. Repetitive motion, like cutting, carrying full buckets, or laying brick, increases the chance of getting them, and well-fitting gloves can be a real asset in keeping them from occurring.

Extensive exposure to mortar, cement, concrete and the like is very drying to the skin. How many of us have had the ends of our fingers literally split apart from being so dry? Or cuticles that catch and tear, or just start bleeding? Gloves (and keeping our hands clean) will help prevent this from happening. It may seem "girly" to care about your skin, but when you're slowed down on the job because your skin is so dry it's bleeding, you'll wish you'd taken better care.

Tool Safety

Scratches and dry skin are one thing. Near-amputations are another entirely. NO ONE wants that, for themselves or their co-workers.

Tool safety starts before the job begins. Are you using the right tool for the job? Screwdrivers aren't good replacements for hammers, and vice versa. Take the 2 minutes, walk back to the van, and get the right tool for the task at hand. If your work vehicle doesn't carry the right tools, ask your employer to get them and make them available.

Are they strong enough? You wouldn't fish for tuna with a rod meant for trout, so don't use 'homeowner' type tools when a professional grade is required.

Check the tool's condition – are they in good repair; no cracks, splits, loose components? Do they feel like they are coming apart in your hand?

If it's a power tool, how does it sound? Any unusual noise or vibration when it's turned on? Any loose or worn components – is your blade sharp and clean, is the drill bit secure? An incorrectly functioning power tool can break your arm or take a finger off, even if you are wearing PPE. More and more, tool manufacturers are offering battery-powered tools, eliminating the need to haul extension cords around a work site. However, you need to remember that both the corded tools and the cordless variety carry quite a punch, and you have to be prepared.

A lot of folks scoff at reading the owner's manual or operator instructions – 'I've been around tools all my life; I don't need someone to tell me how to run a Skilsaw.' But tool manufacturers, just like any other manufacturer, strive to improve their products. You need to read the manuals; you need to keep them handy so others can read them too. That doesn't mean you have to fill the work vehicle with paper; keep digital copies available for easy reference for all the members of your team. Those manuals will, usually, include the date of manufacture, any sort of service recommendations, and possibly an expiration date. This is all information you need to reduce your risk of damage or injury.

You may have team members who haven't come from a construction background. Maybe they didn't even grow up in a family where everyday maintenance and repairs were done, all that sort of thing was hired out instead. So, they are coming from a real lack of common sense about tools. You could say, "they don't know what they don't know." They lack a basic aptitude that comes from a lack of exposure. That is not to say they can't learn; they could become some of your best workers – you certainly won't have to break any bad habits! But you need to be responsible, you need to make sure they are trained properly, and that they have the chance to ask questions and get comfortable with all the tools you expect them to operate. They should not just be trained on how to use the tools; they need to learn how to maintain them, and what kinds of injuries they can cause. They need to learn what to look out for.

That training includes proper care. Have you ever seen someone walking around a job site, carrying a power tool by the cord? Or have you seen a frayed and damaged cord that's been loaded up with electrical tape? It's true, good tools are expensive, and you hate to get rid of one over a bad cord. But that is not only a safety hazard; it can violate federal health and safety standards.

We've seen people disable the blade guard in order to get into a tight spot, or try to cut a board while holding it, instead of clamping it on a secure surface. We've seen people fail to unplug a drill before changing bits, or use dull or bent bits instead of going back to the van for a new one. They aren't being deliberately careless. Usually, it's a combination of complacency and laziness – when you've made a thousand cuts, or drilled a thousand holes, it's not uncommon to let your mind wander while you're doing it, or rationalize that it's 'just this once'. And why not make one simple hole, even though the bit bent? You've done it over and over, and most of the time you get away with it. But that's not how you maintain a high safety standard for yourself or the people around you.

Pants

When it's 90 degrees out and the humidity is way up there, most folks want to wear shorts. Certainly, it can be a lot more comfortable than long pants.

But if we're sweeping chimneys or working in certain types of job sites, we're exposed to all kinds of carcinogens. That material can get up the legs of our shorts and find its way to places on our bodies where, quite frankly, nobody wants to think about having cancer. Soot and dust are remarkably able to get up around all sorts of spots on our bodies. When you get home at night and shower, what color is the water? For many of us the answer would be "black" or "gray". Now just think about that stuff, those carcinogens, settling in all over you, penetrating your skin.

Long pants, in the dog days of summer, are not comfortable. But they provide you with a greater level of protection, not just from soot and other troublesome particulate, but from skin injuries as well. A good pair of double-front work pants, like Carhartt's®, can be the difference between a bad scratch and a visit to the ER for stitches. Many types of work pants also have a pocket built in for knee pads, so you don't have to deal with straps around your legs, the pads slipping, or them making it hard to walk around. That gives you another advantage in terms of using protective gear, and may make you more likely to actually use them.

Recently, one of the authors received a very deep cut due to wearing shorts in a warehouse. If I had been wearing long pants, it is likely the cut would not have occurred, or certainly not been as severe.

Protective Clothing

Tyvek® suits are not designed for comfort. They're kind of like wearing your own personal sauna. No one really "likes" wearing them.

But consider this: one of us had to climb around in a large crawl space recently; it was full of dust and soot and debris. I was in 'full gear' – suit with a full hood, boots, gloves, and a mask. When I got home that night, guess what? I had a little debris on my face, but the rest of me, despite being in this filthy, dusty, dirty space, was clean. Without that suit and the rest of it, no way would I even consider doing that job.

It's easier to work in these suits if you aren't feeling confined, so we suggest buying the largest suit you can reasonably move in (if you're a really small person, you may not want the XXXL size, but definitely something much bigger than you normally wear). You want to be able to twist, turn, roll, and not have the suit pull free of the gloves or boots or bind you up so you can barely move.

Now, this isn't the kind of thing you put on in the morning and wear all day long. Many folks don't use them for the average job, they pull them out for the 'big ones', like the job discussed above. They're disposable and they're cheap, so at the end of job you pull it off and toss it. Personally, they make us feel protected, definitely worth the relatively minor discomfort they cause. And when you get home at the end of the day and realize you look like you barely did anything, you know you took care of yourself, you protected yourself.

These are, basically, biohazard suits. When a restoration company has to deal with a dead body in a home, this is what they wear. We encounter dead animals in our line of work – birds, mice, raccoons, squirrels. They get into chimneys, or in the dead space behind a wall, fall in a well or cistern, get trapped, and die. They are biohazards, and we need to protect ourselves, as they carry disease that can be transmitted to humans.

If you're approaching the work area on a job site, one that has maybe just been opened, or a fireplace that you're about to sweep, and start to smell something rotted (we all know that smell), we need to get out the Tyvek suit and protect ourselves. Cleaning off the smoke shelf, or doing demolition for a home remodel, we may find the remains of one or several dead critters. Nobody wants to touch them, and we definitely want to get rid of them as quickly as possible.

Knees

Contractors, including builders, plumbers, and chimney sweeps, end up on their knees on many (or even most) jobs. Sometimes we're down there for 20-30 minutes – or longer - at a stretch. And what happens when we stand up? If you're 18, 20 years old, you may just 'pop up' after kneeling for an hour. But for most of us, stiff legs are the result; we have to 'walk off' the kneeling before we can be comfortable. Our knees don't have any sort of built-in padding; in fact, they are about the 'boniest' part of our bodies, and they aren't engineered to bear that kind of weight directly.

What sort of surfaces do we encounter in our daily work? Soft, deep carpeting? No – we are on brick, tile, stone, plywood decking. Materials that exacerbate the discomfort of being on your knees.

The easiest, smartest way to protect your knees is to wear knee pads. You should consider putting them on to be part of your routine, just like putting on your gloves. You can invest in a pair of really good knee pads that will last, or you can get the cheaper ones that you will have to replace pretty often. The other consideration is the better-quality ones have straps that go around your calves or thighs, and fully cover your knees. They stay put; you don't have to fidget around with them, you don't have to adjust your pants constantly. And as we mentioned above, there are brands of work pants that have pockets for knee pads built right in. You don't even have to take them off between jobs; you can wear them all day long.

Even the good ones will wear out; you are putting a lot of pressure on them, and the padding will compress over time. Still, they last a lot longer than the cheap-o kind. No matter what kind you use, pay attention to their condition and replace them when they aren't doing the job the way they're meant to.

While knees can be replaced, no one wants to go through that ordeal. Knee pads won't guarantee you will never need a knee replacement, but they will definitely help you avoid it.

Shoes

There are a few different considerations that come into play when discussing footwear. You may find you need to have options, have more than one type of shoe, sometimes even on the same day.

Regardless of the type of shoe you use, this is not the place to save a few bucks. Invest in the best quality shoe or boot you can. Make sure they support your feet, allow you to traverse the work surface safely, and are going to stand up to the kind of use and abuse our lines of work include. And they have to fit right; how long would you last on the job in shoes that pinched or squeezed your feet or, possibly worse, were too big, so your foot slops around inside with no support? Take the time, spend the money, and get the right footwear that fits right.

For most of us, having a shoe that grips well on a variety of surfaces is key. Crepe gum sole shoes or sneakers with good tread are your best bet for roofs; Cougar Paws are a good quality brand that offer great traction, even on wet roofs. You do <u>not</u> want to wear leather-soled shoes on a roof! You also don't want to wear that old pair of sneakers that are so worn out that you can slip 'n slide on them.

Other situations will require other solutions. If you're working on a construction site, steel-toed boots may be desirable, or even mandatory. Oftentimes, these boots are heavy, even clunky, and may not be a good choice for going up and down a ladder. This is why you may find you need to have footwear options available to you, from day to day what you need can be different, and one pair or style of shoe may not do it all.

The other advantage to a good pair of boots is the ankle support they provide. If you are walking the peaks and valleys on roofs, or traversing an unfinished floor, a simple misstep can give you a sprained ankle. Boots with good ankle support, whether they are work boots or more of a hiking type boot, are a good option to have, especially if you have some weakness there.

If you are sweeping a chimney, or taping and mudding an interior wall, you may do just as well with sneakers. They will allow you to get around easily and, in the summer, are going to be more comfortable than a heavier boot. You still need to protect your feet, but you don't need a full-on work boot for days like this.

Finally, if you work in the northern part of the country, you are going to have to contend with cold, wet, snowy weather. If your feet are cold, you are going to be miserable; it doesn't matter how warm your body is – if your feet aren't warm, nothing else will matter. So, in addition to the right shoe or boot, be sure you wear warm socks that wick the moisture away from your feet so they don't end up feeling wet and clammy.

You are on your feet all day – you have to protect them.

NOTES:

Chapter 5: Working Conditions & Materials Management

Warehouse Safety

In visiting a lot of businesses around the country, one thing we've noticed is, quite often, the warehouse is a menagerie and an invitation to safety failures.

People using shelves to climb instead of bringing over a ladder and setting it properly, pushing materials off a high shelf instead of carrying them down, climbing over stuff because materials aren't put away properly – it's a recipe for disaster. In addition to the potential financial loss from materials being damaged and becoming unusable, all these sorts of shortcuts increase the risk of injury, from cuts and scrapes to things like broken bones or head injuries from falls.

Again, prevention is the key. Properly laying out the warehouse, storing materials correctly, providing the right tools for people to get to the materials, and having those tools readily available, is essential if we are to prevent accidents and injuries. This means having a variety of ladders, based on where material is stored. If you have shelving that is 15-20 feet off the ground, you need ladders that will get your people up there safely. You also need shorter ladders, for those materials that are stored above the warehouse floor but low enough that the taller ladder isn't the right choice for reaching them. Your people should not have to improvise to get what they need from the warehouse.

Forklifts

A quick note about forklifts: they are not golf carts. They have large blind spots. They should have a back-up horn or alarm. They can tip over; they can run through things. This is heavy equipment and it takes zero time to run through and destroy a stack of product. You have to be very aware of your surroundings – how close you are to materials, people, and the shop dog. And they are NOT a substitute for a ladder or lift – don't hoist someone up to grab something. Tell them to take a minute and grab the right sized ladder for the job.

Forklifts can run on different power sources; electric or some type of fuel, like gas, diesel, or propane. If it is fuel-powered, you need to check it regularly for leaks. In either case, they need routine maintenance, they need to be checked to make sure nothing is loose. When not in use, they need to be parked on a level surface and, if there is one, the emergency brake needs to be set. If there is no emergency brake, chock the wheels to lock the equipment in place. Whoever in your company is expected to drive it has to be trained and certified in the operation of the equipment.

Proper Lifting

"Lift with your legs, not with your back." How many times have we all heard this? But how often do we ignore it? "This isn't heavy, I can just grab it." "I've been working out - this is a piece of cake for me." Well, maybe. Maybe you can get away with it. Or maybe, you will hurt your back in such a way that you are limited for the rest of your life. It's really amazing how easy it is to do serious harm to your back.

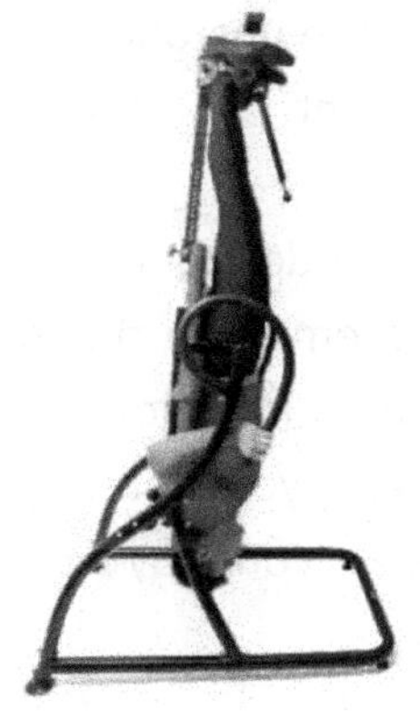

We also need to think about what we are lifting. If something weighs more than 80 lbs, you should not be trying to lift that alone. Yes, most of us can actually lift more than that, but a lot of what we work with is awkwardly shaped, which puts its center of gravity out in front of us, where we can't get it in close to our own. This isn't the gym; we aren't weight training. We are trying to ensure that our bodies will stand up to the demands of our jobs for decades. This means more than just avoiding strain, we need to actively 'support' our backs. One tool some of us use is an inversion table or teeter. You lay into the table, hook your feet in, and flip it so your head is down and feet are up. It helps lengthen and straighten the spine, and keeps your body loose. It may seem gimmicky, but our teams have found it very helpful, and we have one right at the shop. Don't knock it 'til you try it!

Your warehouse tools aren't just for delivering and pulling material from their storage locations – you also need to consider how those materials are moved around the warehouse floor and out to your vehicles to be delivered to the job site. Lifting straps transfer the load to your shoulders, so you can use the full strength of your body to lift. You need carts or a heavy-duty lift for transporting heavier materials, pallet jacks for parts that come on pallets, possibly even a forklift if your operation is large enough to warrant it. All these tools take strain off your body, which not only reduces the risk of injury but also helps stave off the kinds of wear-and-tear damage that takes its toll on us over time. Look at your warehouse the way a risk manager would: what's the worst thing that could happen to someone who tried to move materials in and out of storage? Are things balanced precariously on high shelves, where they could fall on someone's head? Are sharp materials, like cut sheet metal, stored in such a way that those edges are exposed, possibly even in a way that a person walking by could be cut? Are materials stacked higher than recommended, so they are unstable and could fall? These are all considerations you should look at.

The warehouse layout should be clear and easy to understand; you don't want people tripping over stuff, and you want them to be able to find what they are looking for quickly and with the minimum amount of effort. Tape out sections of the floor and label them, label your shelving, making it clear what goes where. For larger operations, you may want to have a 'map' of the warehouse and have it posted in a number of locations.

Workplace safety extends beyond the job site. It's all the aspects of your job, including where and how you store your materials. This doesn't just apply to the 10-truck company with a 20,000 square foot warehouse; even if you are storing stuff in one half of your garage, it should be done in a way that maximizes safety – for you and your materials.

Welding or Torch Protection

Whether you are putting things together (welding) or taking them apart (plasma cutters), you need to fully protect your body.

The use of cutting equipment can burn your retinas. Additionally, you will have sparks flying around, which can burn not just your skin but your eyes too. You can't just 'squint and look', you have to actually protect your eyes. A welding mask gives you really good protection for your eyes, for your whole head. Notice in the photo, left; this person is wearing, not just a welding mask, but a hard hat, respirator, and a head sock. That respirator is important; you aren't just making sparks. You're creating dust, stuff you don't want to be breathing in. These tools can also generate a lot of noise, so you want to protect your hearing as well. Even inside a helmet, it's a good practice to use some sort of hearing protection.

One thing to keep in mind when you're wearing a welding helmet; you can't really see what's around you. Both plasma cutters and welders generate sparks that are hot enough to start a fire. When you're working in one of these helmets, make sure any combustible material is moved out of the area or, if that isn't possible, have a 'spotter', someone who can watch the area around you (from a distance), looking out for ignited material.

Look at the image again. Is there any visible skin anywhere? No. Every inch is protected. In addition to the helmet and respirator, their entire head is covered; they are wearing long sleeves and heavy gloves. Which is a good thing – plasma cutters can reach temperatures of over 40,000 degrees F – literally as hot as the sun. Sparks from welders can be as hot as 2,500 degrees F. Not as hot as a plasma cutter, but still enough to cause serious pain. It should go without saying that this is no place to cut corners – you want to buy the best quality protective gear you can find. You want it to last a really long time, and you want it to truly protect you, day in and day out.

Disorganized Work Vehicle

When I visit people and open their work vans, I sometimes get quite a shock. The inside of the van is a disaster area; tools and materials are all over the place, things aren't secure, and honestly, I don't know how they find anything in there. A disorganized work vehicle is just an invitation to bad things happening. Keeping your truck or van neat, clean, and well organized creates a safer work environment and will allow you to do your job with less risk and greater efficiency.

It's not just organization for organization's sake. Your work vehicle is your 'on-the-go' work space and warehouse. Lack of organization is a safety hazard. Having to climb over loose equipment to get to what you need just invites injury. And having things loose in your van while you're driving is a really bad idea; do any of us want to get clobbered by some tool or piece of pipe that comes at us in a sudden stop? Even if you have a divider, so those objects aren't getting to you, they are still flying around. We carry ten, twenty thousand dollars' worth of tools and equipment on a daily basis. What happens to that stuff, if it's not secured, in an accident? Do you really want to replace things just because you have a disorganized and unsafe van?

Now, most work vans have a divider, so the driver and passenger are protected. But some of us install a bucket seat in the back – a five-gallon bucket that the third guy sits on on the way to a job site. What happens to him in an accident, or even when there's a sudden stop? Five-gallon bucket seats are simply a really bad idea.

Even something as simple as a dirty windshield can be a driving hazard. One of us wears glasses. I will sometimes get into a rental car where the inside windshield hasn't been cleaned properly. That can cause a tremendous amount of glare, and it can be deadly. People have been killed in accidents caused by glare off a dirty windshield. So, it's not just about cleanliness, it's about your safety.

Your truck should be neat, it should be clean, it should be organized. This is your work space. There should be a walkway through the van so you can reach every drawer and shelf without having to climb over stuff. "A place for everything, and everything in its place." What good is having the latest and greatest tools if you have to spend 15 minutes pawing through random buckets and shelves, trying to find something you "just know" is in there? And how much more likely is it that your crew will not use the right tool, or wear the proper safety gear, if they can't find it? If the job calls for heavy gloves but you don't know where they are, isn't it likely you'll do without 'just this once'? It doesn't do us any good to have all this safety gear if you can't lay your hands on it when you need it. It just encourages people to skip using it.

In terms of organization, it makes sense to keep the things you use the most together, in an easily accessible spot. You are grabbing those tools 5, 10, times a day, so you don't want them buried deep in the van, where you have to climb in and out repeatedly. You want them by a door, and together, so you can reach in easily. This is supported by the science of ergonomics and it not only saves time, it reduces body strain.

Maintaining the organization in your van only takes a few extra minutes every day. You have to put things back where they belong; you have to wipe down any gear that will suffer from being dirty. It's so much easier to do this as you go instead of a monthly 'deep clean' (which only lasts for a day or two anyway). Creating good habits while being organized saves time and lessens the potential for injuries.

Often a company will invest in a Lean expert* to design and 'Lean out' the interior of their work trucks. This is an exceptional idea that can have a big payback in reduced injuries and waste reduction. However, the challenge that faces each manager is sustaining the goal condition of the work truck. It requires ongoing inspection, audits and accountability; if you allow it to return to poor condition, then you are the real problem.

Your truck is also your business card. Would you hand someone a dirty, stained, torn card? Of course not. But you pull up their driveway, you open the door to the back, and your customer is getting an eyeful. What are they thinking when they see it? Personally, I would be concerned about how you are going to treat my home, if you display so little concern for your tools and equipment.

Even if it's not 'your' van, you should still take pride in your workspace. As an employer, it doesn't feel very good to see your property, things you've spend tens of thousands of dollars on, treated like junk. Badly stored tools and materials are more likely to break, more likely to be damaged. Another consideration is that it's very difficult to track whether anything has been stolen from your van, or left behind on a job site, if it's in a constant state of disarray. How do you know if that brand-new drill is missing if you don't know where to find it? You may only discover theft when you need something and it's nowhere to be found. You can look into an organized van and see pretty plainly if something isn't there.

** Lean is a process of organization that applies of all segments of a business; its intention is to eliminate waste in all ways, converting waste dollars into value dollars. Understanding and implementation of Lean principles will benefit both the persons working in the truck and the company. For more information, go to: https://www.lean.org.*

Ladder Stowage and Access

None of us want to drive down the highway, look in the rearview mirror, and see our ladders bouncing in the road. Certainly, we don't want to have to replace them, but what about the hazard we have caused? What if someone is hurt, or worse? This is a nightmare scenario, but one that happens all too often. Ladders need to be secured to the racks; they need to be chained or secured in place. You can't just count on gravity to keep them on the racks. And the chains or bungees you use have to be inspected regularly and replaced if there's any sign of fatigue or failure. It costs so little to replace a tie-down system, but costs so much if it fails at a critical time. And if you are on an interstate highway, you have to meet DOT specifications, part of which is properly securing the load.

In today's world there have been many advancements made in the area of truck and van ladder racks; they offer both a secure stowage and can reduce the dangers of a back or other bodily injury in stowing and removing a ladder from the ladder rack. Are they expensive, yes, but the added features make it worthwhile. However, keep in mind these require periodic maintenance; neglecting that will negate the added value they provide to you and your workers.

A lot of companies are using tall vans now, the kind in which you can stand up. There is a lot about that that is good; it's much easier on our bodies to not have to crouch our way in and out of the van. But that also means we need a way to get those ladders down, a way that is safe and reduces the chances of injuring ourselves in the process. Many have a drop-down feature, so you aren't actually reaching to the top of that very tall van. But you still need to be aware of the mechanics of lifting; there has to be a system. You have to have your body in the right position, where you can bear the weight and get it up over your head without pulling a muscle or having the ladder slip and knock you on the head. You may be doing it five or more times a day. Some of these ladders are rated for 250 to 300 lbs; these are not cheap, flimsy things. We've even seen guys climb up the FRONT of the van, walking on the windshield, and step onto the roof! If you're lucky you'll just have a dented roof, but think about what could happen if someone were to slip and fall from there.

Another feature of these high-top type vans is there is room inside to store your smaller ladders. You can store the stepladder, and even an extension ladder, inside. They are easier to stow and remove, and they aren't exposed to the elements, which can help with longevity.

Some people work out of pickup trucks, where the ladders actually hang off the end of the vehicle. These have to be marked, and the driver has to always be aware of the extra length when maneuvering in traffic, backing up, etc. They are a safety risk and particular care needs to be taken to prevent harm to the ladder and anything around you.

Most of us could not do our jobs without ladders. While we may not need them for every job, we will need them often. Just like any other tool, they need to be stored and secured appropriately, to protect both our investment and the people and objects around us. OSHA has specific guidelines regarding ladder damage and longevity; you should be familiar with them and incorporate them into your business standards.

Extension Cords

Extension cords, or drop cords as they are called in some parts of the country, are another essential piece of equipment. A good quality extension cord is not going to be cheap; you need something that can handle the voltage you will be putting through it, so it gives you the power you need. No "Christmas tree" cords! And it should have a ground fault circuit, to trip power if something goes wrong.

Whether you have a 10-foot or 100-foot cord, it needs to be stored properly. That means coiled up and secured. You don't want to spend 5 minutes on a job site untangling a cord that was bunched up and thrown into the van. You can get wire cuffs to help properly secure them between uses.

Another reason to properly store these cords is it helps protect them from failure. You don't want to put a lot of stress and strain on the junction point of the plug or receptacle end and the cord itself, or create tight kinks in the wire that are vulnerable to damage. An extension cord 'repaired' with electrical tape violates OSHA standards and could get you in trouble, as well as increase the potential for injury. Nobody wants to get shocked – or receive a large fine.

If you see the cord is frayed or damaged, bite the bullet and replace the cord or, if the damage is at the junction of the cord and the plug or receptacle, do a proper repair. You can cut the cord below the problem spot and install a new end. Make sure it's grounded, it's tight, and the screws are good. You want to replace the end with a comparable part, something that will keep it in conformance with federal and state guidelines.

Power Lines

In some parts of the country, power lines are buried, so there's one less thing to be concerned about as you work off the ground or on the roof.

But most of us see power lines running to the houses we are going to service. And that means we have to be very aware and plan our work space and approach carefully.

We always want to put our ladders up correctly, so they stay in place. "Correctly" is more than just having the base on secure ground. We also want to survey the area around the ladder, top to bottom. Of course, we never want our ladders to slide; we want to set them properly and ensure they are stable. But were something to go wrong, we wouldn't want it to be made that much worse by coming in contact with the power service.

We have to take the time to walk all the way around the house, look at access from every side, and make sure we are protecting ourselves. We've talked about making sure we set our ladder at a spot that gives us the best access to the roof, where we won't damage landscaping, or where we won't be over an uneven or unstable location. But we also need to look for the power lines, where they connect to the house, and plan to avoid those as well.

It's not uncommon to see the power entering the house in very close proximity to the chimney. If you need to work on or around the chimney, see if you can approach the chimney from another direction, so your ladder is set safely away from the lines. If not, you need to have the homeowner contact their electric company to come out and wrap the lines with insulated blankets. That way if, God forbid, something touches them, it comes in contact with the blanket and not the power lines themselves. Sometimes, the power has to be shut off, but in most cases the blankets do a good enough job that, coupled with our staying alert and aware of the risk, we can work in their vicinity safely. Once your work is complete, and the ladders or scaffolding have been taken down, the homeowner can have the power company turn the power back on or remove the blankets.

Before you even take the ladder off the van, walk the property. You aren't just looking for the best roof access, or how to avoid the point where the lines connect to the house, you're also looking up. You're assessing where you can walk with your ladder, particularly if you are carrying it vertically. This applies to setting your scaffolding as well. Before you carry pieces through the property, or start to set everything up, make sure you are giving those lines a proper berth.

Fiberglass ladders don't conduct electricity, but they are usually a lot heavier than aluminum ladders. As your aluminum ladders need to be replaced, it may make sense to get at least a few fiberglass ones. You should be aware that there are now much lighter fiberglass ladders on the market that were developed for the telecommunications injury, due to the property damage and injuries that are associated with a heavy fiberglass ladder.

You've found a good spot to set your ladder, you're up on the roof, and you need to get a closer look at something near the lines. Use the zoom on your camera, take some pictures, and view things that way. Don't be a hero and get in close to the lines – bad things can happen.

There is also a danger when there are foggy conditions and you are around power lines. Electricity can travel through the fog, so if fog is present you may need to rethink your safety precautions to accommodate this. There have been industry fatalities traced to this; don't become a statistic.

There has been one incident we are aware of, in which someone was killed by the arcing of electricity. Scaffolding had been erected close to the power line. The power arced to the scaffolding, and there were two workers on it at the time. The person who was higher up on the scaffolding survived; the person lower down, who was standing on the ground with his hand on the scaffolding at the time, was electrocuted and died. Give yourselves room.

Appliances and 110 Voltage

At some point in our lives, all of us have gotten an electric shock. It's usually more startling and unpleasant than truly dangerous, but it depends on the amps running through whatever it was that gave us that shock.

Most homes are filled with electrical appliances, and our work may bring us in contact with those appliances and/or the home's wiring. Pellet stoves, appliances, and appliance blowers run on electricity, and they all have the ability to shock you.

This is a weird situation, but demonstrates what we can be dealing with when it comes to electricity. There was a retail stove shop with a tin roof. A metal factory-built chimney servicing a woodstove ran up through this roof, and the woodstove had a blower on it. One day, someone had to go on the roof, and it was hot – not 'temperature' hot, but 'power' hot. There were 110 volts from this motor, and somehow there was a short; it traveled through the stove, up that metal chimney and to the roof. Now who would expect that could happen?

The range of possible injury from electricity is broad. Exposure to one amp will usually cause a 'tingle'; five amps will feel like what we would call 'a shock', more disturbing than painful. But as little as six to thirty amps can cause loss of muscle control and can make a person 'freeze', to not be able to let go. Imagine that happening to you on a ladder. The shock would be painful but it could also lead to more severe injuries from the fall it caused. And if the current is strong enough, you can experience heart arrythmias, severe burns, cardiac arrest (heart attack), even death.

We will see different circuits with different amps in the average home. If you look in the breaker box, you will find 10, 20, even 30 amps, and you can find voltage of 110, 220, and possibly 440, running through there. You will want to have a device for checking the voltage.

Your plasma cutter, spot welder, or other high voltage equipment may run on 220-volt. This higher voltage increases the chances of severe injury or death, and the appropriate safety steps must be employed. Anyone operating these tools must read, understand, and follow the manufacturer's safety guidelines to ensure you and your people are protected from such risk.

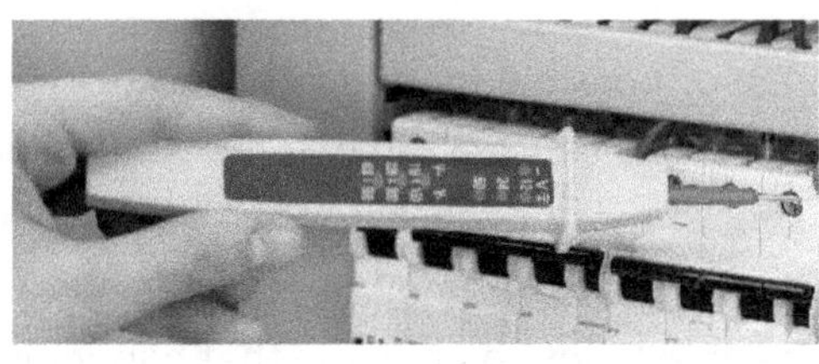

A multimeter (above, left) will give you a read of the actual voltage. A voltage tester (above, right) is typical of the type used by home inspectors, to test how many volts are running through a particular circuit.

We know of an electrician who worked in a printing plant. He always kept his left hand in his pocket when screwing in a screw. When asked about it, he explained that, if he held anything else, he could ground himself and be killed.

Although you wouldn't usually associate woodstoves with electricity, they can have blowers with 110 current running through them. Pellet stoves typically require electricity to operate; you touch the wrong thing and you can blow the circuit board. So, the first thing you must do before working on any powered appliance is unplug it. If you forget, then touch something and hear a "pop", that can really scare the heck out of you. If you're lucky, you just blew a fuse. If you're not so lucky, and you're working on a pellet stove, you could've fried the motherboard. This is not a cheap repair – you could be out three, four hundred bucks. All it takes is remembering to always unplug powered appliances, and you can avoid that very unpleasant and expensive mistake. Capacitors store energy; make sure they are discharged or disconnected before starting service.

NOTES:

Chapter 6: Job Site & Roof Access

Gravity always wins. So, you need to make sure you don't give gravity that chance. The farther you fall, the worse the landing is going to be. The farther off the ground you are working, the greater the risk – but we know of workers who have received fatal injuries from falls of less than ten feet. Protecting yourself and your crew from ANY fall is critical.

Ladders

We have multiple options when it comes to ladders – step, extension, telescoping, straight, multi-way. They each have a purpose, and in our line of work we will need many, if not all, of these. Your employees should have safety training, initial and remedial, on every type of ladder you provide, including knowing the appropriate use for each.

Training should include

- which type of ladder to use in a given scenario
- safety ratings for each ladder type; does it have the capacity you need?
- can it carry your weight as well as the weight of whatever you are carrying?
- how to identify the material a ladder is made from (aluminum v. fiberglass, for example)
- the proper way to carry, set, secure, and store each type of ladder

All training should be documented, and this should include subject matter, date, instructor, and participants.

Before you step foot on a ladder, you need to know how to take it down from the work vehicle, how to carry and set it, proper distance from the structure it will rest on, how many rungs should be above the point of contact, how to check its stability, how to come off and back on the ladder, how to take it down, and how to store it on the vehicle. You should have someone watch you perform each of these tasks the first few times, to make sure you aren't overlooking something. The correct way to do things isn't always obvious, and it's a lot easier to develop the right habits from the start than to un-learn the wrong ones.

You also need to be able to tell when a ladder should be taken out of service. If the rope on an extension ladder is frayed, the pulley system is bent or failing, the rungs are broken, the rung locks are broken or bent, the feet are loose or bent (among other things), the ladder needs to be repaired, if not replaced. Even though there is no expiration date on a ladder, you need to check for cracking (fiberglass ladders) or warping (aluminum ladders). In some cases, and depending on the degree and type of damage, we are expected to tag a ladder as out of service at this point. And if you are an employee, you need to make sure you inspect the ladders you use regularly, and report any damage or failure to your employer. Unless they are working side-by-side with you in the field, you can't expect them to know about this – you have to speak up. They can't provide the right equipment if they don't know.

Fiberglass ladders do not conduct electricity, right? Well, if they are dirty enough, that soot/dirt/slime can, and now that ladder you "know" isn't an electrical hazard has become one. So, keeping the ladders clean becomes a pretty important safety requirement.

Ladder Accessories

We now have a variety of tools and attachments that decrease our risk when using ladders. Even if we only use them sporadically, each has a definite value when it comes to making ladder use safer.

Before you purchase or use any of these accessories, make sure you understand their function and how to employ them on the job.

Fall protection ladder extension. This device allows you to climb through the top of the ladder onto the roof, instead of going around one or the other of the legs. The transition from the ladder to the roof, then from the roof to the ladder, are the more dangerous aspects of ladder use. This attachment can make that transition less risky. It also gives you that little extra bit of height for those times when the ladder is not quite tall enough.

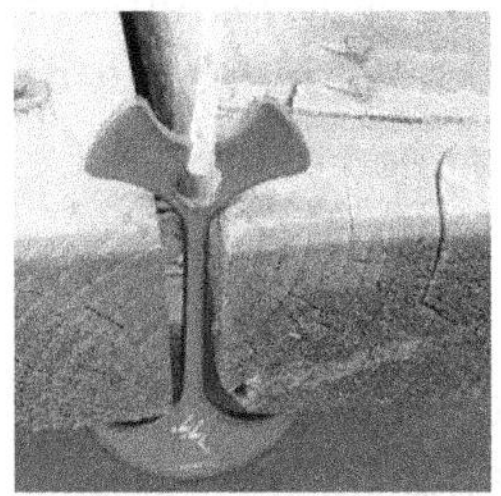

Deck anchor system. Sometimes we have to set our ladders on a wooden deck, which is not an ideal scenario. These anchors are pushed down between the boards of the deck and twisted so they 'lock' in place, then use ties to secure the anchors to the ladder.

Ridge hooks. The ridge hook does just what its name implies: it is attached to a ladder, then the hook goes over the roof's ridge to secure that ladder on the roof. Typically, they include a wheel to guide the ladder up the roof without having to drag or push it, possibly causing damage to the roofing material. The wheel swivels freely, so you may find your ladder starts to veer off to the left or right as you send it up. Now, all of sudden, your ladder is going off at an angle, possibly even towards those power lines you have been so careful to avoid. So, many people immobilize the swivel function, allowing it to only travel in one direction. This gives you a lot more control over where the ladder goes, and saves you from having to 'muscle' a misbehaving ladder into place.

Leg levelers. We can't always find level or nearly level ground on which to set our ladders. This tool allows us to, basically, make each ladder leg a different length to compensate for the ground where we've set up.

Ladder grip or ladder stabilizer. One of a ladder's worst enemies is wind. You can set up in a great spot, get those legs nice and square, you think life is good. Up the ladder you go, then onto the roof. A huge gust of wind comes along; the next thing you know you're hollering for the homeowner to come rescue you. These devices attach to the gutter quickly and can save you from having to find your way off the roof when the ladder ends up laying in the yard. There are similar products that attach to the roof when you don't have gutters to use.

Goat Steep Assist. This is actually a replacement for a roof ladder. The sections lock together, and there's a soft hook pad that goes over the ridge. It includes hand/foot holds, which you use to climb up and down the roof in a small footprint.

You may need to use more than one tool at a time, depending on the situation. And there may be times when you are using more than one ladder at a time; you need every one of them to be set up and secured properly. There was an inn that had a chimney that was too tall to reach from the roof. A chimney sweep brought a stepladder to the roof, set it against the chimney, and climbed up. On his way down, the ladder slid out from under him. In the fall, he ruptured his Achilles tendon and was laid up for 4 months. A simple tie off on that step ladder would've saved him a lot of time and pain.

Scaffolding

A scaffolding system, properly erected, is one of the best, safest ways to access the rooftop, including the top of the chimney. It's usually quicker to go up and down scaffolding than a lift, and it provides a flat surface on which to work. It's also very useful when dealing with fragile roofing material, like cedar shake or slate, allowing you to avoid the risk of damaging it.

When you are on a big project, where you are on the roof for days, it doesn't make sense to work from a ladder or the roof itself. Standing on an angle for hours on end, such as when you are working off a roof surface, is brutal on your body. You feel it in your legs, your ankles, your back. And that stress and strain, over time, can become a chronic problem. While it might not shorten your life, it can definitely interfere with your ability to enjoy yourself as you age.

Before you use scaffolding, you need to be educated. There are multiple OSHA regulations and standards that you must adhere to. You can't just cob parts together; you need something that meets OSHA standards, and that has been engineered and tested. You have no way of knowing what a home-built system can hold; do you really want to send three or four guys up there, without knowing whether it can handle the weight?

Even with an OSHA-compliant system, you need to know how to put it up. If you haven't been taught how to do this, there are classes available. It's worth the investment. And once set up, there should be a competent person on-site throughout the job; in case something goes wrong, they will know how to address it.

Another consideration with scaffolding is what is involved in setting it up and taking it down. These are not usually a one- or even two-person operations. Look at the picture on the left; that is a complex setup, made even more challenging by the shake roof; they couldn't attach into the roof itself so the structure is essentially self-stabilizing and supporting. In other conditions, you can use chimney scaffolding frame brackets, which have a wide range of adjustment so you can create a level work surface on most roofs, regardless of pitch. These can be used in conjunction with peak hooks, attached to the planks holding the scaffolding and to the roof ridge.

You don't want to go to the trouble of erecting something like this and use junk parts. If a component is rusty or bent, if a weld has failed, cut it up. If it seems like it's broken, it probably is. Make sure no one is going to find that part and try to use it again. Tag it out and get rid of it. As expensive as new scaffolding may be, it's cheap compared to the harm poor scaffolding can do, to your customer's property and to you and your crew.

Once it's up, the safety concerns aren't over. Almost every time, scaffolding is going to be in place for a number of days, or even weeks on a really big job. You need to mark off the base and the area around it, and make it inaccessible to people besides the ones hired and trained to work there. Scaffolding can be an 'attractive nuisance', inspiring neighborhood kids to check it out. You need to do due diligence to prevent that. Your work vehicles should carry safety tape, safety chains, and traffic cones. Use the tape or chains to mark of an area around the scaffolding to alert passers-by of the potential risk and the need to keep their distance. If your work brings you close to (or even on) a roadway, use traffic cones to caution drivers going by that they are passing an active work site and should drive accordingly.

You also need have processes in place for how workers and materials are moved to the top of the scaffolding. Moving brick, stone, mortar, roofing shingles and the like is hard, physically exhausting work; moving it to the top of your scaffolding is even more demanding. In a later section we will discuss some ways of doing this that will afford you and your crew a greater level of safety.

You just built a tower in the air; it needs to be secured correctly to the structure itself. Most of the time, you're going to encounter wind at some point in the job. If the top is wrapped, maybe to protect the unfinished work, you've basically added a sail to the tower. That is a tremendous increase in surface area that wind is going to act on, so you need to be sure that structure is as stable as you can make it.

Properly erected scaffolding, simply put, makes your life easier. A job can be thirty or forty feet off the ground, but you can have a level, stable work surface, one that allows you to keep your tools and materials at hand, and inflicts the least possible stress and strain on your body.

Lifts

Another way to get workers and materials up to the roof is with a lift. These are becoming more popular, and we find chimney sweeps, masons, painters, and roofers are making the investment to own one; alternatively, you can frequently find them for rent.

The purchase price on a lift can easily be a six-figure investment. In addition to the purchase price, you need to calculate the cost of the system you will use to move it from place to place; will you need a more robust truck to tow it, or can your current work vehicle handle the load? Will you need a trailer?

There are different types and sizes of lifts. The more versatile is the articulating lift. It can bend in the middle, which will allow you to get up and out, over a roof, which gives you far more flexibility. You can get 60-, 80-, even 100-foot lifts, which sounds like a ridiculous size. But consider that that represents your total vertical and horizontal reach. A large "McMansion" could easily require that. One of us had a job on a little one-story house. Simple, right? Except there was a brand-new metal roof, and the owner didn't want it touched. With the articulating lift, we could complete the job without an issue, and make the customer very happy.

Lifts are not like driving a car; you will need to be trained. Some have controls in the basket; some in the basket and also on the base. Some are driven and others must be placed in position by hand or with a vehicle. This is not the kind of thing you want to 'learn by doing'; take the time to learn all the functions of the lift you will be using, and remember that they aren't identical; you may need to re-train if you're using one you haven't operated before.

Another consideration is their weight; one of these things can really chew up a yard or driveway. Can you picture Mr. Homeowner as you casually drive over his beautiful lawn, leaving giant tread marks? None of us wants to face that. Get heavy-duty plastic or rubber mats to lay over any surface you wish to protect. You will need a few of them; you can put two down, drive over the first onto the second, move the first in front of the lift, and sort of 'hopscotch' across the yard that way. You will want to keep the lift on one of these pads as you are working, and lay plywood or some other sturdy material under the outriggers that may be used to stabilize it.

Before you drive onto a property, ask the owner to point out any underground structures, like a septic or irrigation system. Having to replace someone's septic tank or lawn sprinkler system is expensive and doesn't reflect well on you. Get the customer's permission for where you need to go to access the job.

Know the limitations of the equipment you're using. The baskets have a maximum weight capacity. Make sure you don't exceed it, and make you to take into account the workers AND the materials. It's tempting, when you are trying to make as few trips up as possible, to keep loading more material, brick by brick or shingles, bundle by bundle. And remember that the max weight extended and un-extended will be different. So, you may be fine going straight up; then you have to extend 15-20-25 feet out over the roof. Is it going to withstand that stress? Or are you at risk of toppling over onto the roof?

While in the basket, you need to be harnessed in. Although your lift will allow you to work from a level and fairly stable surface, you are still exposed to potential hazards. A bad gust of wind, leaning just a little too far to avoid having to move the lift, overextending the arm – all of these can leave you vulnerable to a fall.

Lifts can make it possible for you to take on jobs that would be close to impossible without them. While purchasing one may not be in the cards for you, finding a reliable rental source for one can open up many options for you and your company.

Material Hoists – Manual & Electric

As we mentioned before, moving materials up to the work area can be very hard on the body. Even a 'young buck' is going to feel it after carrying bundles of shingles or buckets of mortar up a ladder or scaffolding for hours at a time. And a lift, while more convenient, is going to need a lot of trips to get everything to the roof on a larger job. So, what's another way to get what you need where you need it?

Use a material hoisting system. A well pulley attaches to scaffolding; the bucket is filled, the worker at the bottom pulls down to raise the bucket. Our worker at the top takes the material from the bucket and it is lowered, then the cycle is repeated.

There seems to be a threshold for hoisting materials manually; most worker's bodies would start to give out at about 35'. What we would do is have 2 workers at the bottom; the first would hoist to where they felt they were going to lose strength, then the second person would take over. This protected those people on the ground from having the load slip and come crashing down towards them.

A few (major) concerns for the workers at the base of the scaffolding:
One – you need to wear safety gear; you need your helmet and your gloves. Rope burns are painful, and in a worst-case scenario you can lose a finger. Wearing eye protection is a must as well; any debris that's coming off the bucket or the scaffolding can get right in your eyes.
Two – your equipment should be in excellent condition. Check the rope; it should not be frayed or broken. Check the welds, the hook, the condition of the pulley wheel. If anything looks 'iffy', replace it.

Three – when you are pulling on the rope, you have to pull DOWN. It may seem easier to walk away from the scaffolding, so you can engage your legs in the process, as well as not having to move the rope in your hands. But what happens to the scaffolding itself when you pull out? You are creating an angular force, substantially increasing the risk of pulling the scaffolding over with you. This may not make much difference if the scaffolding is fifteen feet tall. What if it's fifty feet instead? That's a tremendous amount of angular force, enough that it can destabilize the tower.

An alternative to this manual system is an electric hoist. Instead of manpower, it uses a motor. They usually include a swivel arm, so the materials can rise up on the side of the scaffolding, then the arm is turned inward so the worker at the top can unload everything without leaning out and putting themselves at risk. Some have a conveyor belt that runs along a top-most section of the lift arm, bringing materials over the roof to the job site.

Walking on Roofs

Just like the ground, roofs have a variety of 'terrain'. Walking in a valley or along the peak are going to be easier than walking a steeply pitched area.

According to OSHA, you are required to use fall protection, such as guard rails, safety nets, or personal fall protection, when you are working more than four feet off the ground. The exceptions are 1) if you are on a ladder and 2) if you are "inspecting, investigating, or assessing work or workplace conditions prior to beginning work or after all work has been completed." There is a mistaken belief that there is a time exception to this rule, that if you are only going to be on the roof for 5, 10, 15 minutes, you can forego fall protection. This is not correct. And to be clear – "inspecting" as noted above does not refer to an inspection job. If you were hired to perform a chimney inspection, for example, you are required to use fall protection. The inspecting, investigating, and assessing referred to above describes a situation where you are on the roof to gather information for a work proposal, so you are not actually "working" in the sense that you are not performing a service or repair.

However, even at those times where fall protection is not required, consider carefully whether this is a situation where it just makes sense to use it. You do not have to do the bare minimum required by OSHA; when it comes to keeping yourself and your coworkers safe, going above and beyond is a good policy to follow.

This presents an interesting question – if you are working on the highest part of a building, where do you secure yourself? You need to know what is required by law, and you need to be prepared to adhere to those standards. That means you have to own the type of equipment that is needed to meet the standard.

Fall Protection

At the start of this manual, we talked about assessing a job site. That assessment should include potential hazards and dangers on the site. This review should be standard operating procedure for every company, and the results should be considered when preparing the proposal.

The number one cause of injury in industrial and commercial work is falls. Safety boards, both OSHA state and federal, are focusing on this now. So we, as contractors, should be focusing on the elimination of hazards, both to avoid OSHA investigations and, more importantly, to keep ourselves and our employees safe. We all need to be aware that OSHA regulators are doing drive-by inspections. There is no warning, and they are issuing large fines when they see violations. In other words, Big Brother is watching!

There are 5 general types of fall protection:

-Hazard elimination – remove or minimize exposure to potential falls

-Passive – physical barriers, like guardrails on scaffolding

-Fall restraint systems – harnesses that restrict range of movement

-Fall arrest systems – equipment that prevents a fall of a certain distance, reducing potential force

-Administrative – practices or procedures that increase worker's awareness of risk

Ropes & Harnesses

One form of fall protection employs a lanyard attached to your back, then connected to a stable point. They act similarly to a seat belt, in that they will 'snap you back' if you try to extend them past their maximum length. Other times they are a fixed length, and the length is set so you cannot get past the edge of the roof and fall.

Different forms of fall protection are frequently used in conjunction with one another. Even when wearing harnesses, you will find the perimeter of the roof flagged so there's an obvious, physical 'sign' denoting the outline of the work area.

Some companies, particularly when working in a high-traffic area, use them on every job. You don't want to draw attention to the fact that your company may use them selectively.
Regardless of how often they are used, every work vehicle should have enough harnesses for all the workers it carries when it goes out each day. Ideally, each employee should have their own harness, fitted to them. While it may be a challenge to get in the habit of using them, repetition will make it become second nature over time, which benefits everyone.

Twenty years ago, with the exception of some really large job sites, you rarely saw workers wearing harnesses. But as we became more aware of the risks, and the number of fatalities became better known, their use became more common. Within the chimney service industry, there are two gentlemen who have really led the way in teaching on this subject – Bob Ferrari and Jim Brewer. Because it isn't just a matter of putting a harness on and climbing up on the roof; the harness should be fitted correctly, designed for the use in question, and be comfortable. An improper harness can injure you, especially if it lacks the appropriate shock-absorbing value. A harness that fits poorly, or is uncomfortable, is a harness that won't get worn.

Do not mix and match parts from different fall protection systems; don't pull a strap from one kit and use it on another harness. You wouldn't put a Honda part on a Chevy – treat your safety equipment the same way.

The next factor to consider is the rope. This is, literally, your lifeline. You don't want one that can stretch past the point where you will hit the ground! It has to be strong enough to support your weight and then some; you don't want a rope that is 'just' strong enough.

Your harness and rope need to be inspected regularly. This is the gear that is preventing a massive and/or life-threatening injury. Is your rope fraying? Does it have worn or weak sections? Are any of the connection points on the harness loose? Any worn straps? You need to discard anything that's damaged; saving a little money by holding onto safety gear past its useful life is a huge – and unnecessary – risk.

Your gear needs to be kept clean; it needs to be stored properly so it isn't being abused. It should be kept in a closed container, like a bucket with a well-fitting lid, to keep dirt, dust, and debris out. Keep the containers secure in the work vehicle, not rolling around and in the way.

This is a really brief overview of this topic. You should make the investment in getting the proper training in selection, fitting, and use of harnesses and other safety devices. Our point here is to make you aware of the hazards you may encounter, and to encourage you to get more specific training in these areas, to protect yourself and your team.

The Elements – Weather Conditions

Most of our work is done outdoors, and even if it's not, we have to travel to job sites daily. So, we have to deal with the elements – ice, wind, snow, rain, heat – every day. Every one of these has the potential to harm us, from increasing the risk of car accidents, to slips and falls, to heat stroke.

Some of this goes back to how you take care of yourself. If it's hot, humid, or very windy, you need to stay on top of your hydration. You need to be clear-headed when driving or walking in snow, wind, and rain. And in all conditions, you need to dress for the weather; layers are always a good approach, so you can adjust and adapt when things change over the course of a day.

If your business is in the northern part of the country, you are undoubtedly working in snowy conditions at some point. Even a few inches of snow down south will cause a company to shut down for a bit, but in the north, you have to figure out how to work with it or go out of business. That's not to say that northern businesses don't shut down in blizzard or white-outs. But under 'regular' winter conditions, the show, as they say, must go on.

Another consideration is that we frequently need to be prepared to shovel snow. Shoveling is strenuous exercise, and it's not at all uncommon for it to bring on heat exhaustion or even a heart attack.

You want to be sure you keep your shop yard shoveled, salted, and de-iced, so you don't have people slipping and falling before heading out for the day. Your drivers should take the time to remove ALL the snow and ice from the vehicles before heading out for the day; in some states it is actually illegal to drive with accumulation on your roof. These laws came into being because not removing snow and ice from your vehicle can lead to serious accidents, injury or death to people or vehicles with whom you share the road. Imagine a huge chunk of ice flying off and smashing into the car behind you. Not a pretty sight.

Working in the heat brings its own set of issues. Heat exhaustion and heat stroke are very real health concerns; heat stroke can kill you. You need to work out of the sun if at all possible; wear a hat, HYDRATE, and use sunscreen. Use easy-ups or pop-up covers over your ground work or staging space. It can be 10-15 degrees cooler under a cover than standing out in full sun.

NOTES: ____

____

____

____

____

____

____

____

____

Chapter 7: Vehicle Safety

Driving Safety

When we talk about job safety, one area that is often overlooked is driving safety. Defensive driving – scanning for potential problems, watching the other vehicles on the road and staying ready to react, being aware of weather conditions and how they are affecting road conditions – is essential if you are going to avoid problems behind the wheel. Even if you drive well, you know there are plenty of idiots out there, so you need to drive in a way that protects you from them. You can't count on them looking out for you.

Being able to drive defensively goes back to taking care of ourselves; we need to be rested, get proper nutrition and hydration. We need to keep our vehicles, especially our windshields, clean and clear.

Weather conditions can change suddenly and with little warning. You could leave the shop in the morning, with clear skies, then have a storm come up during the day. All of a sudden, you're heading home on flooded highways, and risk your vehicle – or one right near you - hydroplaning. In some parts of the country, roads flood quickly. You can't just drive through; you need to look. If you can't see the roadway under the flooded spot, don't go there. It doesn't matter if it means driving 30 minutes out of your way to find a safer route home. It's worth it.

Wind, rain, and snow can come up quickly. You may find yourself on a leaf covered road in a torrential downpour. Those leaves are going to be slick and it becomes very easy to lose control of the van or truck. Severe thunderstorms make driving trying in the extreme; sudden snow squalls can catch you unawares. Staying in contact with the office, letting them know you are running late, or even that your day has to end early, is important, and will relieve some of the stress that being caught in bad weather can bring. There's no job that's worth an accident; you can always reschedule.

There's also the issue of what it's like to drive a work vehicle. Our newer employees, in particular, may not be familiar with how a heavily-laden, top-heavy vehicle performs on the road. It may sound funny, but you need to have them take some laps around the parking lot to get a feel for how the vehicle responds to the brakes, how it corners, what it's like to back it up. Most of them don't have a center rear view mirror, and they often have huge blind spots. Do you really want to back into a customer's yard or driveway without having a sense of what that's going to involve? Without knowing what sort of blind spot you're dealing with? Best practice would be to invest in having backup cameras installed on all work vehicles. Elimination of one accident will pay for the camera.

Another new experience for many of us is towing a trailer or other equipment, such as the tow-behind lifts we discussed earlier. There are a host of other considerations when you have something behind you. It affects how you change lanes, accelerate and brake, how you navigate a corner, and how you back up. You also need to be mindful of trailer lights; you have to make sure everything is connected properly and the lights are working, so the drivers around you know what you're about to do. You must consider the gross vehicle weight (GVW) of the truck, trailer, and load to comply with DOT requirements and applicable driver's license endorsements.

You may be driving with ladders up top, some of which may overhang the front or back of your vehicle. You have to flag those correctly, and take that extra length into consideration when you're navigating.

Tire pressure is something many folks overlook. You need to check that regularly, especially in a heavily laden work vehicle or trailer. Blowing a tire, especially on a trailer, is not something any of us want to deal with. The thing about trailers is they aren't usually used every day; they tend to sit around. So, you may think the tires are good, but there's some dry rot going on and/or the tire pressure is low, which leaves them susceptible to failure. For the small investment of time it takes, check your tire pressure regularly. It's also a good practice to replace tires on any work trailers prior to dry rot setting in and creating an opportunity for tire failure.

Texting & Cell Phone Use

Texting and driving – we've all done it at some point. We know we shouldn't, we know it's not the smart thing to do. And if road conditions are poor, it's an even worse idea. How many times have we heard of an accident happening while the person was texting? Too many.

On the other hand, we need to stay in contact with our office, and pulling over for every communication (voice or text) isn't always practical. Bluetooth, hands-free devices give you that freedom without sacrificing your safety. You can keep the office and your customers updated about whether you're running late (or early). Now, many of us have jobs that run multiple days, so we aren't seeing several customers a day, but for those of us who do keeping them apprised as to when they will see us is just good customer service.

More and more people use texting nowadays; you can shoot a quick text to a customer to let them know when you expect to arrive. It's probably easiest to send that text as you're finishing the previous job, before you get back on the road. But things come up – accidents happen, road work is underway, things that we don't expect end up delaying us.

You can set your phone in the dash holder, where you can see it but don't have to touch it. Several states (and more every year) are "hands free" – use of handheld devices is illegal. Getting caught on your phone can get you a ticket and cost you points on your license. If you're setting up the GPS on your phone and the police officer thinks you're making a call, you're getting that ticket – they don't care. Newer vehicles have Bluetooth built in, so you can synch your phone to the vehicle's sound system and do everything by voice command.

Several states now have roadside pullovers specifically set up to encourage people to get off the road to text or call. After we started losing people in accidents, states figured out that something had to be done. "Everything" is an emergency, people feel like they have to answer every text or call. Having these pullovers recognizes that people aren't going to ignore their phones; the pullovers are a better, safer option. But even if there isn't a designated pullover spot, you need to find a place you can safely get out of traffic if you're going to answer a call or a text.

NOTES:____

Chapter 8: Animal Hazards

Insects That Sting

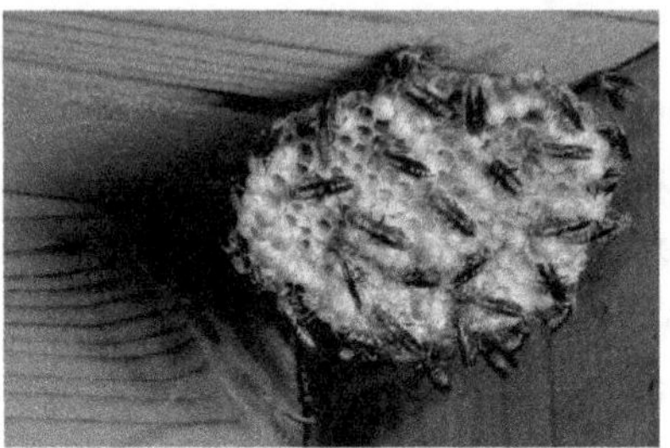

Now we're going to talk about critters – critters that bite and critters that sting. This includes wasps, hornets, yellow jackets, honey bees, and fire ants.

Even if you've been stung in the past, you need to be aware that you can develop an allergy, and your reaction can be severe enough that you can go into anaphylactic shock. This causes your airway to swell and close up and requires immediate medical intervention. If you have had a reaction in the past, you may be eligible to get an EpiPen. If not, at minimum you should carry Benadryl or another, comparable antihistamine.

Insects like these can nest under chase covers, in roof eaves, in the ground, and inside structures you may need to dismantle. Before you get into an area you can't visualize, bang on it and stand back; you will most likely see something flying out. Always have wasp and hornet spray on hand. Stand back and spray the area thoroughly. There may be times when you have to repeat the process a few times to make sure you've gotten them all and now have a safe area in which to work.

Critters That Bite

Insects aren't the only things to look out for; animals can bite too. And not just 'the wild things'; you need to be wary of pets. Animals of all kinds will bite in self-defense; they will bite if they perceive something as prey.

Many of us know a service tech who has been bitten by 'a dog that never bites'. So, instead of being a never-biter they are now a first-time biter. And you don't want to be the person that became their first victim. It's not uncommon for a technician to be bitten more than once by one of these 'first-time biters'.

Very few homeowners will tell you their dog bites. Usually they will say, 'oh, he's very friendly' or 'he just wants to sniff you'. But it's always better to be safe than sorry. Whenever you have to work inside someone's home, and they have a dog, ask that it be secured in another room. Particularly if you are working with loud tools, like drills, vacuums and the like; you won't know that dog is behind you until you feel the bite. Bare minimum, keep something between you and the dog; a vacuum, piece of furniture, something that affords you some protection and gives you time to react.

When you arrive at a house, be prepared for the possibility that there is a dog there. When you knock on the door, stand back and be prepared. Some dogs have been known to charge the door, ready to attack. And don't walk around back and go through the gate to look at the far side of the house without altering the owner first; you could be walking right into Fido's pen. Always keep your eyes open and have an escape route planned. We like to carry a heavy mag-like flashlight whenever we get out of the work van. If absolutely necessary, it can be used for self-defense. The owner is not going to like it, but if a dog is coming at you, snarling and teeth bared, you have a right to protect yourself. Statistically, you are more likely to be bitten by a small dog than a large one, so don't let their cuteness fool you!

While it's not as common a risk, the family cat can scratch, claw, or bite you as well. It's just a good plan to treat any unknown animal as having the potential to harm you, and act accordingly.

Insects That Bite

Ticks, spiders, lice, mosquitos, bed bugs, and fleas bite, and many carry diseases. Spiders, like the black widow or brown recluse, have bites that inject you with poison that, in some cases, can kill you.

Mosquito or flea bites are usually more an annoyance than anything else; you get an itch, maybe a bump, but you rarely need medical attention.

Most of our work will not bring us in close contact with bed bugs, but they have been known to hide behind loose wallpaper, in the crevices between cushions on upholstered furniture, even behind picture frames on a wall. Again, their bite is not usually more than a nuisance, but they like to 'hitchhike' and you may find yourself bringing them home! Likewise, head lice can travel from person to person if there's close contact, so it's very unlikely that you will be close enough to a customer to be affected.

Tick bites are another matter. Lyme disease and Rocky Mounted spotted fever are the most well-known tick-borne illnesses, but they also transmit babesiosis, ehrlichiosis, anaplasmosis, Southern Tick-Associated Rash Illness, Tick-Borne Relapsing Fever, and tularemia. They are particularly common in the northeast, and you can pick them up just walking through a wooded area or high grass. Even a low pile of brush in the yard can harbor ticks. If you've spent any time outdoors, especially if you've been around tall grass or wooded spots, you need to check your body head-to-toe when you get home at night. It usually takes them being attached to you for over 24 hours before you contract an illness, so that daily check is really important.

Spiders are everywhere. They hang out in pretty much any area where they are unlikely to be disturbed, like old, unused chimneys, under decks and porches, and in attics or crawl spaces. We need to be cautious and not reach into spaces we haven't visually inspected. Shine your flashlight all around before you stick an arm in there. As we mentioned before, there are poisonous spiders, whose bite can cause you some serious medical issues. So, take your time and do that visual inspection first.

Critters That Carry Rabies

Rabies is found in every state in the continental US, and is carried by a variety of animals. Bats, raccoons, skunks, and fox are the most common carriers; small animals like squirrels, rats, chipmunks, and rabbits rarely carry the disease. Opossum, interestingly enough, are remarkably resistant to rabies. Their 'bluff routine' mimics rabies' symptoms, which is why some people claim to have seen rabid opossum. Unvaccinated domestic animals can carry the disease, but that is the exception rather than the rule.

If you are bitten and the animal can't be captured and quarantined, you will be treated as though you have rabies. This used to involve several shots in your stomach, which was not at all pleasant. Nowadays, the shots are given in your arm; still no fun, but better than it used to be.

Untreated rabies is almost invariably fatal, so regardless of how much you hate needles, you need to go through with it.

We once saw an entire work force shut down by a rabid raccoon in the midst of the work vehicles, and all work stopped until animal control arrived to remove the animal.

Generally, when we find a wild animal in an area in which we are working, we stop, contact animal control, and let them take care of it. Sometimes, though, we discover the critter once we are really in there. In those cases being prepared, by wearing our protective gear and being well covered, will protect us to a large extent.

Animal & Bird Droppings

Even if the animal itself isn't around, we still need to be aware of diseases that are carried in their droppings. It's not unusual for a variety of wild animals to take shelter in and around our homes, whether it's inside the chimney, in the attic, under the roof eaves, or in outbuildings.

The diseases you can contract from droppings can infect you via physical contact or by inhalation. So, in situations where you may encounter this you want to be sure you are protected, you're wearing gloves and even full-body protection, you're wearing your respirator.

In particular, chimney sweeps run into this fairly consistently. The smoke shelf in a fireplace is a common location to encounter droppings, and you've got to disinfect it when you do find anything. You also need to dispose of your vacuum filters after you've cleaned up from this; you don't want to spread anything around.

If your job takes you into attics you have probably discovered, at some point, piles of droppings from birds or bats. It is also common to encounter them on roofs or on the outsides of chimneys. Before you get into any sort of repair or upgrade, you need to disinfect any areas with signs of the stuff, then take whatever was used in the cleanup and dispose of it properly. You don't want to go to work around this stuff, so if you find it during the initial walk-through for a job, be sure to include the cost of cleaning in your proposals, whether that's new vacuum filters, extra labor, or even hiring a specialist to remove it.

According to Google, there are forty-two different diseases that can be spread through contact, physical or airborne, with animal waste. Legionnaire's disease, rabies, West Nile virus, E-coli contamination, and histoplasmosis are probably the best known, but there are more.

NOTES: ____

____

____

____

____

____

____

____

____

____

____

____

Chapter 9: Material Safety Information

Material Safety Data Sheets

A few years ago, many of us in the trades had little awareness of material safety data sheets (MSDS). However, more and more often you will find companies have a full binder of them in the office as well as on the work vehicles, covering virtually every product workers may come in contact with. The MSDS cover all the ingredients, what they're used for, what they do, and the manufacturer.

If someone ingests something, the MSDS is of critical importance. The sheet can be given to the ambulance crew or ER doctor so they know what they're dealing with, which means your employee or co-worker will get the correct treatment. It literally could be the difference between life and death. You do not want to be sitting in the emergency room after 5 pm, trying to reach a supplier to find out what's in their product; you want that information at hand. It's something you never want to have to use, but are so grateful to have should the need arise.

Everything from a can of spray paint, to different types of mortar, to water repellent, to adhesives, you name it, there's a MSDS. And you need to have sheets specific to the brand and type of material you are working with; spray paint from one company may not have the same ingredients or require the same medical treatment as the same product from another company.

Hazard Communication Standard

In addition to the MSDS, you will want to label materials in the shop or warehouse. Most all of us have seen these diamond-shaped hazard signs, whether on tanker trucks carrying them on the highway or on supplier's shelves.

The hazards are broken down by class – class 1 is explosives, class 2 is gasses, 3 is flammable liquids, 4 is flammable solids, 5 is oxidizers, 6 is toxic materials, 7 is radioactive materials, 8 is corrosive materials, and 9 is miscellaneous dangerous goods. From there, signs can include a sub-type of material and be labeled 5.1, 2.2, etc.

Labelling these materials correctly is federally mandated. Usually, the containers holding these products will come with the correct markings, but it's really your responsibility to make sure that's the case. Especially if someone decides to transfer the contents to another container, maybe they need a small amount, then put it back on the shelf – and now it's unmarked. You have to stay on top of that, make sure your employees know what is supposed to happen when materials are moved from their original container.

NOTES: ____

____

____

____

____

____

Chapter 10: First Aid & Personal Care

First Aid Kits

Every work vehicle, warehouse, shop, and office should be equipped with a quality first aid kit, and replenished as supplies are used. A lot of the products in a kit have expiration dates, and those items should be replaced as they hit that date. Note: Any work vehicle over 10,000 lbs. GVW must comply with DOT State and Federal First Aid and Safety Equipment.

Most contractors will need to have, at minimum, kits that include a variety of bandages, gauze, tape, eye wash, burn cream, butterflies, ice packs, antiseptic and antibiotic creams, and tweezers. The kit should be kept handy, but not somewhere it will get stepped on, kicked around, or otherwise abused. We have found tucking it behind the driver's seat in the work van or truck keeps it close at hand but also protected.

A first aid kit is not going to take the place of an ambulance or ER in a major accident, but it may make it so you can keep someone alive until that help arrives. Get good quality kits, keep them replenished and up-to-date. This is not something to skimp on.

Stress & Burnout

A lot of people find discussing mental and emotional health difficult. There is still a stigma attached to these subjects, but thankfully that's starting to change. Stress can be overwhelming and it can take a physical toll.

When the busy season hits (which, for some of us, is a year-round thing), the phone is ringing off the hook, materials aren't arriving as promised, everyone needs you NOW. How do you deal with this?

It starts with taking care of yourself; getting the right nutrition, hydration, rest, and exercise. You want to do everything you can to get yourself into optimal condition, not just physically but mentally. It won't stop the stress from happening, but it will make you better able to cope with it. Even with that, sometimes you need to just walk away – step away from the phones, get off the job site, take a little walk and clear your head.

Burnout is another big problem. This is when you just want to throw your hands up, give up – it's just not fun anymore. When things are starting to get to you – don't wait until you can't take anymore – you need to communicate; you need to tell your employer, your co-worker, the people you rely on. Let them know; don't try to resolve this by yourself.

One thing we've noticed about burnout: people who are burnt out become careless, and careless people have more accidents. You're not paying attention, your mind is caught up in this pressure, and that's when you get hurt.

Everyone, from the business owner to the new guy on the truck, has responsibilities. We all strive to meet them, but it's hard sometimes, it's stressful. The work we do is not easy. We try to enjoy ourselves, have some laughs with our crew, but sometimes it's not enough. Jobs don't always go the way they're supposed to (in fact, things go wrong at least as much as they go right), things don't arrive on time, parts don't fit together correctly, vehicles break down – these are the facts of life in the service world. And the schedule, particularly in the busy season, is packed, so any misstep impacts not just this job, but the ones after it.

When this happens, it's not unusual for our professionalism to drop. We feel that stress and burnout, we get a little short with people, we don't respond as quickly as we usually do, and our customers notice. That's when it helps to have a good team around you, who can help you see where you're headed and help you deal with the burnout so it doesn't end up hurting your business. Stress and burnout are bound to happen, but how you react to it is important.

Beyond the 'normal' level of stress, some people we are working with may be dealing with mental health issues. If you see someone struggling, do the responsible thing and alert your supervisor or employer. It may feel like you are going to cost this person their job, but their health, and your safety, is more important. Having a co-worker who is not stable, and needs professional help to deal with it, is not where anyone wants or needs to be.

Family Pressures

When work gets crazy busy, our natural inclination is to put in more hours and try to catch up. But we need to be aware of what effect that has on the family – not just ours but our employees too. You need good workers, and you need to respect their personal time. They need to be able to take care of their responsibilities at home – picking kids up from soccer practice, getting to doctor's appointments, and just plain spending time as a family.

Communication is key here. You need to communicate with your family; let them know if you're going to have to work late, or if you're going to need a little extra help on the home front. You need to communicate with your 'work family' too; it's not fair or right to spring long days on people without warning, or add weekend work without giving them a heads up. A good employer treats their employees like team members, and respects their time and effort. No matter how great you are at your job, you can't do it alone. You need your team, and you need your family.

Ultimately, your family is more important than your job. You need to make time for them, get away with them and reconnect. Most of us could not do what we do without that support at home. Make sure you honor it, treat it as the valuable thing it is. If you have kids, or your employees do, you know how fast they grow up. Take the time to go to their baseball games, their band concerts, and make sure you make time for your employees to do the same. It's an old saying, but it's true – these are the days you can't get back. Work will always be there, but your children are young once. Don't miss out on that.

NOTES: ____

____

____

____

____

____

____

____

____

____

____

____

____

Chapter 11: Attitude & Personal Presentation

Overconfident – Cocky

Being mindful of how you conduct yourself is essential if you're going to maintain a sane and safe environment. We see people having accidents, getting hurt, and it's related to how they carry themselves, what's in their heads. Being overconfident and cocky is a quick way to end up injured.

Not always, but many times we will see workers who think they are bulletproof, who think they are superhuman and can't get hurt. They may have done some dangerous things in the past and gotten away with it, so now they think they can continue on that way with no consequences. Often, they won't change until the proverbial bad thing happens, which we never want to see. When we see these workers fall victim to an injury or worse, it is clear they simply took their eyes off the ball.

You can be confident without being cocky. Cocky can make you careless. You may be hitting great sales numbers, racking up the jobs. But if you're cocky, there's a good chance you're going to overlook things, you're going to mis-measure or mis-calculate, and now those sales you made aren't really profitable, or the job isn't done right. And that's exactly what we don't want to have happen.

Lack of Attention to Detail

Systems help us manage the details. Your whole day is made up of little things that add up to a successful day: signing in, getting new batteries to replace the ones that ran down yesterday, reviewing work orders to make sure you load the correct materials in the van for the day, and so on. Having a routine, a system, keeps us from making simple mistakes.

You need to know, the customer doesn't care how you do the job, they don't care about what they can't see. They care about their home, whether you're crushing their favorite rose bush with the scaffolding and whether the carpet is clean when you're done. Some of our work isn't really visible; relining a chimney, for instance, is basically invisible to the customer. You can improve your customer relationships just by paying attention to the little things; are you meticulous around their possessions? Did you make friends with their dog? Did you pick up all the bits of debris on their lawn, or just 'the big stuff'?

Safety comes into play here too. Attention to detail, getting the little things right, is what decreases risk and increases the chance that you and your team are not going to have accidents or injuries.

This goes back to working up a proposal too. Getting photos of, not just the part of the house where work is being done, but the approach to the work area, any potential obstacles, areas that are of special concern to the customer. It includes taking really good notes so when the crew arrives to do the job there aren't any surprises. The salesperson for a job also needs to keep a watchful eye out for any safety issues that will be encountered in performing the repair or the installation, and make note of them for the crew coming out to do the work. You want to set your fellow man or woman up for success, not failure.

A company that has a reputation for taking care of the little things will always be busy. That is the company that gets great reviews, that gets all kinds of word-of-mouth recommendations. Don't you want that to be your company or the company you work for?

Failure to Anticipate What Could Go Wrong

One skill that we often teach in sales training is the skill of anticipation. But anticipation is essential for more than just sales.

We need to 'look down the road', see what could go wrong before it does, so we can avoid the pitfalls before they arrive. Say you're walking across a parking lot in the winter. Is it icy? Are you anticipating that you may fall? Will that change how you walk out there, maybe taking some corrective measures? Part of the skill of avoiding injury is being able to anticipate what may go wrong. This requires clear thinking, which means you're taking care of your body (proper food, hydration, rest) and your mind (managing stress, avoiding burnout).

Getting to the job site and realizing you forgot a critical tool or part is stressful. You've got to waste time retrieving it, your day is going longer, you may be late to the next appointment. You feel like you have to rush, you become careless, now you're not driving defensively, and maybe you rear-end someone because you weren't anticipating that they could stop suddenly. You have to anticipate that someone could pull out in front of you, someone could slam on their brakes.

The other thing that leads to a failure to anticipate is repetition. The longer you do something, like flipping burgers, the more you can go on auto-pilot and maybe aren't as aware of what could happen. Your mind can wander and then you find you've flipped the burger off the grill, or you've gotten a piece of equipment stuck. Especially when you're doing something you've done many times before, you have to anticipate what could go wrong. Crazy things happen every day; stuff breaks that you never thought could, or goes wrong in a way you didn't foresee. All you can do is learn from it so it doesn't happen again.

What you want to watch out for is the snowball effect – one thing goes wrong, then the next, then the next, and it all kind of rolls over you. Eventually, things get pretty bad. So, before that happens, take time to review, to anticipate. When you're pulling materials for a job, consider whether it makes sense to grab extra parts, or different sizes of certain components in case there was an error in measuring. When setting up at the job site, look around and see where the potential trouble spots are, try to anticipate what could happen, and see if you can set up in such a way that you avoid those things happening.

Illegal and Prescription Drugs Use

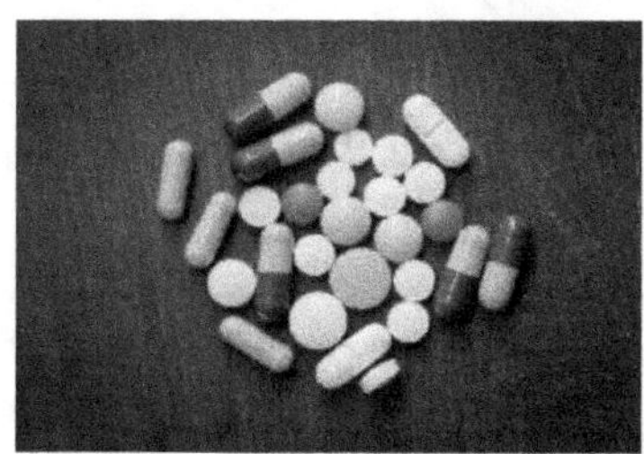

We have all worked with someone, or know someone, who has struggled with illegal, or even legal, drug misuse. It's sad, and hard to talk about, but we have to deal with it if it's going to affect our company and its reputation.

We have had employees in the past who have been involved with illegal drugs and it rarely ends well. They get injured, cause someone else to get hurt, and we have to let them go. Then they lose their families, their careers, and it just spins out of control.

Even worse we have seen drug misuse, whether those drugs are legal or illegal, cause overdose injury or death. Drugs are a very real problem in today's world and we all need to be aware of the danger of improper use.

Whether we know it or not, whether we think it's there or not, we are all going to have to deal with it in our companies. We do everything we can to filter out people with these problems but it's not easy. It's not uncommon for someone who misuses drugs to be able to get to work, function, and act like everything's under control. But we've personally had instances where we are sent a photo of an employee slumped over, passed out on the roof, where he was supposed to be laying brick. Obviously, he's told to get off the roof. Then the next picture was of this same fellow slumped over a bag of mortar in the back of the truck, passed out again. Of course, he no longer works for us. He was a great guy, but he made some bad decisions.

As much as we may wish to be compassionate, with the kind of work we do we have to have zero-tolerance policies in place, and we have to enforce them. Our jobs involve risk, and we can't put other people in jeopardy because one person is a danger.

This doesn't just apply to illegal drugs. Some prescription medication can have a significant impact on your ability to focus, to maintain a stable emotional state, and on how you think. We've all seen people who used completely legal substances that led them to some very dark places. These folks are easily as likely to have an accident, even a fatal one, as someone using illegal drugs.

Personal Hygiene

Don't show up to the job stinking. Personal hygiene, head to toe, is important. Keep beards and mustaches neat and trimmed, keep your hair tidy, keep yourself clean. You are in and out of people's homes and property every day. Sometimes you have to stand closer, to show them photos or such. You shouldn't smell bad doing it. So don't take this lightly.

Yes, most of us can get quite dirty over the course of a work day. This isn't about being 'pretty'; part of taking care of ourselves and our bodies is getting that junk off at the end of the day. Soap and water are your friends. We have had days where we get in the shower and the water just runs black. You don't want that's stuff on your skin any longer than it has to be.

If you're wearing good quality protective clothing, you are going to have much less cleansing to do at the end of the day. We know that on a hot day it can be pretty uncomfortable, and it's easy to make excuses to not wear it. But in the long run it's the healthier choice.

Another thing to consider is jewelry. Watches, necklaces, earrings, rings, plugs, and bracelets can catch on tools and equipment. At minimum, it may hurt a bit and possibly damage your jewelry. At worst, you can end up with a dislocated body part or an avulsion, where the skin is peeled away from your finger. Consider not wearing any jewelry at work, or at least covering it to protect it from getting hung up on things.

You represent the company, whether you own it or work in it, and you don't want to come off scruffy and unkempt. You don't need to go overboard, but staying clean, managing body and breath odors, and keeping your hair, on your head and face, neat, trimmed, and clean helps make a professional impression.

NOTES: ____

____

____

____

____

____

Chapter 12: When Something Goes Wrong

911

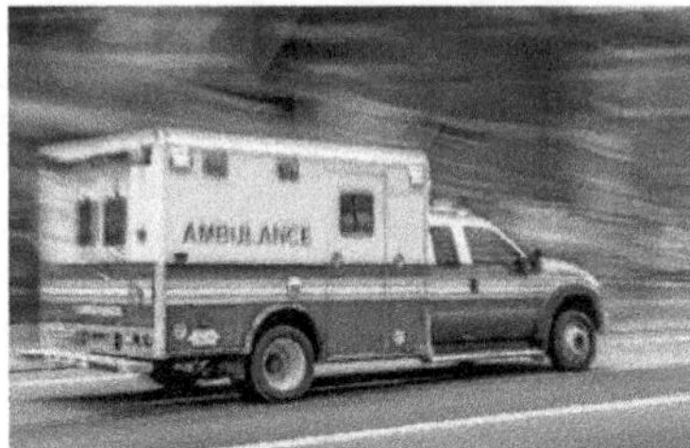

Have you had the 'pleasure' of taking an ambulance ride? One of us had that experience recently; not from an on-the-job injury but from a heart attack. The ride was very smooth, really cushioned, but not one we'd ever want to repeat.

The reason we have invested so much time and energy in this book and course is to help all of you avoid being the person on the stretcher, or the person in the funeral home because, yes, fatalities do occur.

Even business owners who commit to having good safety programs will find gaps or places where improvement is needed. So, if you go through this material and see where you're missing something, take the time now to improve. And if you are an employee, you need to follow those safety protocols and take them seriously. If you find a weak link, share that with your boss. Nobody wants to see someone they know and work with get hurt, and no boss wants that on their conscience.

If you are on a job site and someone needs the ambulance, company policy should be to make that call immediately, then notify your employer or supervisor. You need to stay by that injured person until medical help arrives, you don't leave their side.

One of us was working in a print shop, some years ago, and when there had one of these emergency situations arise:

> I came upon a man lying on the floor, gasping for breath. I was much younger then; I ran out the door and found another guy there and said, 'you've got to come here, this guy's in trouble.' The guy had a big issue and he did die from this particular instance.

I often wondered later; did I react quickly enough? Was there anything I could have done? I wasn't an EMT or a paramedic and I did not know how to care for him in this case.

We aren't suggesting that every contractor needs to have a certified EMT on staff, but remember that knowledge is power. The more you know, the better you will do in an emergency situation. Of course, the best approach is to do everything in your power to prevent accidents and injuries. We hope this has opened your eyes and brought things to the forefront of your mind, so you are able to use foresight and head off those potential accidents before they occur. In fact, we recommend watching the presentation or reading through this book annually, to keep it all fresh in your mind.

NOTES: ____

____

____

____

____

____

____

____

____

____

Afterword

We hope you use this material to develop and implement ways of taking care of yourself (and your crew) that preserve your body and health, that help you prevent those debilitating accidents. It's no fun to get into your later years and be hampered by bad knees, heart problems, breathing issues, and the like. We don't want to see any of you end up needing new knees or a new hip over an accident or careless moment in your youth.

You can be the best carpenter, best mason, best electrician or plumber in the world, and you want to continue to be that for 20-30-40 years. You want to be in good shape so you can keep doing what you're doing and be able to say you kicked its ass, it didn't kick yours.

As the authors of this book and the presenters of the corresponding course (found at www.safetyreviewforaservicetechnician.com), we hope that this information has been helpful to you. We encourage you to make sure every member of your workforce has a copy of this book in their possession and that they take the online course, which is an in-depth class covering the subjects in the book.

Author biographies:

Jerry Isenhour is the founder and CEO of CVC Success Group. He is the author or coauthor of eight books that are distributed by Amazon and through other book sellers. He has operated companies in the service industry, the retail industry, and the manufacturing industry. He has been working as a full-time coach, trainer, speaker, and consultant since 2010, after many years in the business sector. He is certified by the John Maxwell Group, and by Jeffrey Gitomer as a coach, trainer, speaker, and consultant. You can read more about him on the www.cvcsuccessgroup.com and www.jerryisenhour.com. Follow him on social media; he can be found on Facebook at CVC Success Group and on YouTube at CVC Coaching. Jerry has a podcast titled *The Chimney & Fireplace Success Network*.

Feel free to reach out to Jerry at jerry@cvcsuccessgroup.com; he will be glad to schedule a call with you to see if his processes are the processes you need to turn your business dreams into your business realities.

Robby Murphy is the president and co-owner (with his father) of Hudson Valley Chimney in Poughkeepsie, NY. He has worked on the National Chimney Sweep Guild Accreditation Jobs Study as a Subject Matter Expert. He is a Certified Master Chimney Technician who enjoys giving back to the chimney and hearth industry as much as he can. Robby holds his company to a very high standard with the most important aspect being safety. He can be reached at Rmurphy@hudsonvalleychimney.com.

www.ingramcontent.com/pod-product-compliance
Lightning Source LLC
LaVergne TN
LVHW050600160826
845677LV00011B/2384

* 9 7 9 8 3 5 1 3 4 6 7 1 7 *